DUMMY UP AND DEAL

THE GAMBLING STUDIES SERIES

T0097675

DUMMY UP AND DEAL

INSIDE THE CULTURE OF CASINO DEALING

H. LEE BARNES

FOREWORD BY JOHN L. SMITH

UNIVERSITY OF NEVADA PRESS ▲▲ RENO & LAS VEGAS

The Gambling Studies Series

Series Editor: William R. Eadington

University of Nevada Press, Reno, Nevada 89557 USA

www.unpress.nevada.edu

Manufactured in the United States of America

Design by Carrie House

LIBRARY OF CONGRESS CATALOGING-IN-PUBLICATION DATA

Barnes, H. Lee, 1944–

Dummy up and deal : inside the culture of casino

dealing / H. Lee Barnes ; foreword by John L. Smith.

p. cm. — (The gambling studies series)

ISBN 978-0-87417-506-6 (hardcover : alk. paper)

ISBN 978-0-87417-622-3 (pbk. : alk. paper)

ISBN 978-0-87417-550-9 (ebook)

1. Casinos. 2. Casinos—Employees. 3. Gamblers.

4. Gambling. 5. Swindlers and swindling. I. Title.

II. Series.

HV6711 B37 2002

331.2'041795—dc21

2002004785

The paper used in this book meets the requirements
of American National Standard for Information
Sciences—Permanence of Paper for Printed Library
Materials, ANSI Z39.48-1984. Binding materials were
selected for strength and durability.

University of Nevada Press Paperback Edition, 2005

This book has been reproduced as a digital print.

This book is dedicated to my niece Terry and her family—
husband Robert, sons Andrez and Lucas, and daughter Jenna.

CONTENTS

Foreword by John L. Smith   ix

Preface   xv

Introduction: Beyond Pascal   1

1   Breaking In   5

2   Mattress Politics   24

3   Georges, Stiffs, Freaks   43

4   You're Fired, Have a Nice Day   62

5   Cheating   86

6   Coping   104

7   Gambling   121

8   One Dealer's Story   125

Some Afterthoughts on the Text   133

Glossary   135

FOREWORD

SCUFFLING IN SEARCH OF THE REAL LAS VEGAS

There's no shortage of books on Las Vegas these days. If you're hungry to learn about blackjack's basic strategy or the penthouse intrigue of Gaming Inc., you'll have your arms full of suitable selections. At times it seems that every poet, pundit, and college professor is coming out with a take on the city. And who can blame them?

Las Vegas is the place Salvador Dali would have invented if he'd had the money, the spot on the map I long ago dubbed the Second Chance Capital of the World. A generation ago, Las Vegas was where wise guys, racketeers, cross roaders and lammisters traveled to shake off the dust of their old lives and go legitimate—at least as Nevada's legalized gambling was concerned. Today, it's the fastest-growing community in the country, a fact that tickles some locals and frightens the hell out of others.

Las Vegas is an irresistible locale for sociologists, an easy play for pop critics, and nirvana under neon light for investigative reporters. Despite some worthy efforts, most miss the mark. They end up either indicting innocent bystanders or suffering from a whopping case of Stockholm Syndrome. It's not their fault, really. The city isn't as easy as it looks and makes fools of those who trust only their five traditional senses.

One fact that most drive-by experts never fully appreciate is that Las Vegas is the toughest factory town in America. Behind its polished marble floors and larger-than-life themes is the greatest cash-generating machine the world has ever known. Casino dealers, in their deceptively clean black-and-white uniforms and manicured nails, work the assembly line around the clock. Their toil is cleaner than the lot of coal and diamond miners, but the jobs have a lot more in common than you might think. Dealers are essential to the function of the great casino machine, but they are all but nameless, often abused, and easily replaced.

Few writers know the real Las Vegas that exists behind the pulsating facade. Lee Barnes is one.

Forget for a moment that he's a gifted short story writer who is on the faculty of the Community College of Southern Nevada. And although it surely helped him gain the perspective he would one day put to use in Las Vegas, never mind that he is a Vietnam veteran who has worked as a cop and narcotics agent.

As you read this book, remember that he was once a casino dealer who walked through a jungle only slightly less treacherous than the bush he once patrolled as a Green Beret not far from the Laotian border. He was on the front lines, as it were, and he didn't break in soft at one of the Strip's high-end and high-paying carpet joints. Barnes worked downtown, where the lights are bright, the tips are low, and respect is just a song that Aretha Franklin sings.

Although Barnes goes to great lengths to explain that his work is not academic—it lacks footnotes and mathematically precise statistics—it more than makes up for that by capturing the voice and spirit of the ghosts who haunt the casino racket's lower echelon. In that way, its reportorial qualities echo the plight of the "plongeurs" in George Orwell's "Down and Out in Paris and London" with plenty of Studs Terkel's *Working* mixed in. From the boorish bosses to the sex and drugs, it's all here—the real Las Vegas you won't find in any of the corporate revisionist histories or latest travel guides.

In the end, the truth doesn't need footnotes.

This book brings a few long-buried memories surging back. Here's one. I'll never forget my sister, Cathy, excitedly taking the ironing board from the closet and setting it up at the approximate height of a twenty-one table. It was sometime in the early 1970s. She broke out a pack of Bicycles and practiced shuffling up and dealing for hours. I won and lost a phantom fortune across that ironing board. When she could no longer stand to look at the cards, she mucked cheap plastic poker chips purchased from a dime-store shelf. Anyone who learns to manipulate those feather-light checks can easily move the more substantial ones.

Soon enough she was ready for her tryout, which went well. Hell, if you can deal to five players across an ironing board, then working a genuine green-felt table is going from the sandlots to Yankee Stadium. She was as nervous as a schoolgirl on prom night, but I think she also felt a little like an understudy reading for a small part just off Broadway.

There is an undeniable kind of celebrity that accompanies becoming a dealer. The table is something of a small stage, the dealer its spotlighted bit player. She got the job and for several years seemed proud to be on the floor despite the bad hours, constant fog of cigarette smoke, and endless parade of angle-shooting Romeos.

A few years later, I took a seat at her table and watched her manicured hands work in a blur of precision. That coordination is just one of the things players take for granted when they put up their chips. Barnes understands this when he writes, "Dealers simply assume a kind of mistake-free competence in themselves. It's the job, and when one does make a mistake, she's as mystified by it as the customers who witness it. If laborers in other businesses worked as mistake-free as dealers, American industry would be without parallel. It is this extreme measure of competence that makes dealers feel unappreciated."

Unappreciated, indeed. In time, the veneer of glamour wore off like old nail polish for my sister. There were the disputes with chauvinistic supervisors, the two husbands she found and lost on their way to rehab, the chronic wrist and hand problems, clinically known as carpal tunnel syndrome, and the obligatory battle with representatives of the Internal Revenue Service. Oh, how I wish the IRS attacked corporate America with half the zeal it has focused on the lowly card shufflers and dice dealers of Las Vegas. Not even Congress would be able to spend the budget surplus.

The tokes were good, even after taxes, but the job wasn't as simple as remembering to hit on 16 and stand on soft 17. Dealing not only wears out the hands and wrists and turns the lungs to leather, but also coarsens the soul. It's almost impossible not to be affected by the cynicism and desperation that are so often a part of the casino subculture.

Barnes knows the hearts and heads of dealers. He writes of one break-in, "By the end of the week she's gained this much insight: Slave owners were cruel because nothing stopped them from being cruel. She knows if she wants the job, there's a price to pay—insults, dehumanizing comments. The player betting the money is all powerful; the dealer is helpless."

And of another, "She'd actually graduated from college and then dropped out of law school because it disillusioned her, as if dealing wasn't going to disillusion her more. But what did we know?" Like Lee Barnes, who left the grind to pursue his writing career, my sister also got out of the racket, returned to college, and earned a degree in psychology. Today she works with troubled youth in Oregon a million miles from the jungle.

But for every dealer who escapes unscathed, makes the improbable rise through the corporate casino ranks, or finds a sweet gig with a swell boss and fat tokes, there are plenty who get lost in the neon lifestyle. Reading this book will make you wonder why casino dealers have never managed to widely organize their labor into a union capable of negotiating on level footing with management.

One of the unwritten legacies of Las Vegas is its use and abuse of women. The female form has sold countless suckers on the endless possibilities of a Las Vegas vacation. Forget gambling: Nothing markets the city like T&A. Although some women have managed to take advantage of the Vegas rules, that objectification long ago manifested itself in a sort of hybrid superchauvinism that remains in the casino business despite decades of change elsewhere.

Although women have made strides, they still commonly endure the sort of groping and harassment that would result in sweeping litigation almost anywhere else in the country. Barnes touches on this phenomenon, and that fact alone makes his book a worthy addition to anyone's library.

Once in a great while, about as often as a dreamer hits a Megabucks jackpot, the tables are turned. One anecdote gathered by Barnes: "I was on a game the first day Donna was promoted to the floor. She came over as I was bent over the game spreading my deck. She reached down and grabbed one of my cheeks and squeezed. She smiled and said, 'They been doing it to me for years. Now it's my turn.' What's a guy going to do? File harassment charges?"

Fact is, the real Las Vegas is a decidedly politically incorrect world. It takes a certain dark sense of humor to appreciate it, but the pits aren't entirely laugh-free zones. The human condition, as tragic and fragile as it may be, can be pretty comical if you manage not to take it all too seriously. In a city where money is God, those seeking light-heartedness had better search where the stakes are low. Barnes mines gold at Little Caesar's, my tough old friend Gene Maday's cash-generating toilet located across from the now-defunct Dunes and a world away from Caesars Palace. Little Caesar's was a place where gambling degenerates dropped their last handful of pocket change and dealers learned the definition of *dive*.

"One night, so the story went, a man came in and said he was there to remodel," Barnes writes. "He stretched a strip of metallic duct tape over a tear in the rug, pressed it down, and stepped on it. Bingo! Remodeling complete, he left.

"Cabbies get drunk here and lose their money. The joint's owned by a man who also owns two cab companies. He sees nothing ironic in cashing his cab drivers' checks and taking their money in his casino. It's business. But sometimes the cab drivers get down too far; some get buried. This one is down to his last three dollars. He stands, takes two steps back, calls the dealer a string of four-letter names, and heaves three Eisenhower dollars, hitting the break-in's chest."

As misfortune would have it, the break-in is a street-hardened ex-cop who chases the loser down the street and beats him to a pulp. "Two nights later the cabby returns, sits down at the blackjack game, and buys in for forty dollars. It's Little Caesar's. Where else can he play for fifty cents a hand if things go bad? The dealer shakes his head and calls out 'Change forty!'"

Not all the stories in this compelling book end with a simple black eye. One of the rarely published truths about the casino subculture is the fact that it is riddled with a sort of Dantesque dysfunction. For every rollicking Damon Runyon tale, there are a hundred heartbreaking stories that would bring tears to a pimp's eyes. Lee Barnes knows more than his share of them. Thanks to his effort, you'll know a few, too.

Now it's your turn to dummy up—and read. It's time for you to break in and learn something about the real Las Vegas.

JOHN L. SMITH
November 2001, Las Vegas

PREFACE

This book is narrative nonfiction. What is contained in these pages does not and cannot fit into the confines of theory, thesis, and proof. I conducted no surveys to confirm a general representation of attitudes. I have no statistics at my disposal to establish or imply that dealers are more or less unhappy or more or less cynical than other workers—or the opposite, for that matter. I talked to and listened to people and recorded episodes from their and my experience. The weight of this book is carried by stories because they are the interpretive data of daily life and express humanity in a way that cannot be rendered in cold numbers.

I would like to mention the many dealers and game supervisors who openly shared their experiences with me. Those who contributed stories are Tony Badillo, Jeannie Buchanan, Mike Cohen (deceased), Bob Dawson, Louie Goldfinger, Bob Green, Eddie Huffman (deceased), Raleigh Jaynes, Larry Jones, Steve Jones, Alan Lovinger, James Massey, Tonja Page, Jim Prisock, Caroline Presta, Carey Webster, and others who choose to remain anonymous or are part of a collective memory where stories are banked and shared. Thank you very much. Without your stories there would be no book.

Last, I must offer credit to Perry Stewart, who contributed nothing to this book but the title. He died more than a decade ago at a relatively young age, somewhere around thirty, of a heart attack. I dealt craps with him, and he was a good dealer. As I recall he scammed me and others out of about a year's worth of early outs. But that's the nature of dealers, and I hold no hard feelings, especially for the last early out he took. In the break room one day as I sat writing on a legal pad, he claimed that at some future time he was going to write a book about the casinos and intended to name it *Dummy Up and Deal*. A lot of dealers had expressed similar notions to me, but Perry had a title. He might never have written the book, or perhaps he might have had he not taken that last early out. No matter, the title was too right for me to allow it to die with him. For dealers, the expression captures the mentality of the casino business in a way that no other does.

DUMMY UP AND DEAL

INTRODUCTION

BEYOND PASCAL

They are called dealers, which in itself is ironic if we address the several meanings that the word "deal" encompasses. As a verb, "to deal" means "to hand out a portion, to concern one's self with some matter," as in "to deal with pain" and, of course, "to distribute cards in a game." As a noun, "deal" means "treatment received," as in "a raw or a bad deal," and also "an arrangement for mutual advantage." If the house always has the advantage, isn't it a bad deal? Always. Is it a raw deal? Never. P. T. Barnum said it best: a sucker *is* born every minute. Of the many peculiar verging on aberrant behaviors that humans engage in, gambling heads the list because it is an act based on the flimsiest of human emotions—hope (if hope is, in fact, an emotion). Hope flies in the face of reason time after time after time. Slap someone in the face with reason, and he'll beat you over the head with hope. People gamble knowing in advance the imbalance of the odds and expecting to lose. So in this case, the activity well could be an arrangement of mutual benefit. The house wins, the player's expectations are met. Tit for tat. Caught between the varying definitions and the mixture of hope and disappointment is the dealer.

In fact, dealers are merely mediums for chance, conduits through which probabilities find realization—thirty-six numbers and a zero, double-zero on a roulette wheel, and the payoff for one number hit straight up is thirty-five to one. On every spin of the wheel the odds remain true so that over a few hundred spins the house should win two dollars for every thirty-six it returns to the players. That means, in theory, that the players receive 94.7 percent of their money back and the house gets to keep 5.3 percent. In truth, the house retains far more of the players' money than that. In any given month the hold for a roulette wheel might be as high as 30 percent, an amount substantially higher than the raw house advantage of a little over 5 percent. This is called the hold, which is the portion of the money and markers credited to the game minus the amount in chips that leaves a game with players. True, roulette wheels have losing periods but not for long. What this says more than anything else is that Barnum was right about suckers. But the players refuse to see their pictures on a poster with P. T. Barnum pointing at them. Nor can the players see the house. What's the house, after all? A building with carpet and walls and chandeliers? A corporation? What the players see is the dealer.

"How can you do this to me?" a player asks.

The dealer can't pass the blame off onto Blaise Pascal or the player's bad judgment or the house. The dealer must shoulder the responsibility for his or her imagined power, no matter how absurd it is to think that the dealer exercises any control. The dealer becomes not the medium through which chance plays out its pure odds, but rather the conduit of luck. And when the house is hot the dealer's job is to dummy up and deal, and when the house is cold, the dealer's job is to dummy up and deal. Keep the cards flying, move the dice, get a spin in, keep the customer mesmerized. The dealer's art is not the art of Houdini but rather the art of motion. It's fleeting, so fleeting that it goes virtually unnoticed. All that is left to judge it is the outcome—who won, who lost, and how much. The results are the measurement. But the dealers' hand movements are in themselves the real art, a ballet of motion, the laying of cards or cutting of chips or sweeping of a layout—all art, all invisible. What is left after all the motion is the dealer standing behind the table in her uniform. She must face the player.

"How can you do this to me?"

It's easy, chump.

One of the most beautiful sights to watch in a casino is the graceful pitching of the cards and hand movements of a pick-and-pay blackjack dealer. Not a wasted motion anywhere. Watch her holding a deck in her picking hand while turning cards over and in one fluid movement going to the rack with her paying hand and coming out with two colors of chips to pay a winner, then scooping up the dead cards with that hand and moving on to the next bet. It is an art that is already on its way out. The pick-and-pay houses are dying because the new breed of corporate-trained bosses can't follow the action. Cards disappear from the layout too fast. The dealer must hold a deck in one hand and the used cards that she picks up in the other, all the while scooping chips out of her tray. Too much opportunity for theft. One art dying, dying—an art that only an aficionado can appreciate.

Dummy up and deal.

Look at the way cards are fanned over the layout on a dead game. Look at the arc, the general form. Is the lay precise or freewheeling? Each dealer has his own signature. In that neatly fanned-out deck is an expression of who that dealer is. It is subtle. It must be, because there is little room for free-spirited expression in a casino. Dealing is like any work where the worker wears a uniform. The uniform is the first level of all uniformity and the first stage of compromising identity. If the dealer seems like a robot, there's good reason.

Dummy up and deal.

Surrounded by a constant bombardment of noise, enough to shut down the reticular activating system, the dealer often seeks silence inside his head. But silence is impossible. Short of a battlefield, a casino is the most intrusive environment in the world. It's gimmick and blare, flash and glitter, bark and whine. It's a dog baying at three o'clock in the morning, a gun going off in the next neighborhood. It's an odor that burns the eyes. Cigarette, pipe, and cigar smoke drift around the dealers' heads. All manner of human smells converge in the stale, thick air. It's hot; it's cold. Pick the irritant or discomfort, it's there between the red, yellow, and orange carpet and the crystal chandeliers and smoke-stained ceiling. Don't complain.

Dummy up . . . and deal.

And what of the dealers, the instruments of chance? How can we know their experience? Not through the extremes of sociological surveys or movies that romanticize casinos. Their world is too concrete and their experiences too mundane, too tragic, too funny, too human to be well rendered by Hollywood or reduced to statistical charts and baseline figures by some Ph.D. whose nearest experience with dealing was to study a dealer's body language. To understand the world of dealers, we must break through the crust of image and perceptions and hear their stories, understand why these stories endure, and determine what resonates as true.

From the outside looking in, casinos seem all theater—flashing billboards, neck-craning high-rises ribboned in neon, a continuum of human noise that intimates thrill without consequence, if one can afford the tariff. Everywhere you look, the city's an architectural sleight of hand. Theater. It's the ongoing stage inside that the pilgrim seeks, the chance not just to play but also to *play*. Nothing that takes place inside a casino is pure pathos or pure comedy. Ordinary people become saintly benefactors, generous to a fault, or turn into demons that seem to grow hair and fangs, lash out like trapped cats, scream, holler, rage, cry, moan, throw things, throw fits. Name a behavior, and you will witness it in a casino.

Any dealer, if pressed, will admit that the work is like factory work except for the human element; this is where the theater begins. But you have to see the play from the other side of the green felt to actually behold the drama, which is neither a tragedy nor a comedy but rather a blaring panoply of irony and existential interplay, a sort of play of the absurd. Caught between the player's hope and the house's advantage is the dealer, and so he or she is drawn into the play. One of the ironies is that often, like the player, the dealer believes in luck, which is, in fact, nothing more than a series of equations formulated on probabilities of chance.

Although the numbers that dictate outcomes are pure, who among those who sit down at a blackjack or roulette table have heard of Pascal? Sitting at a table is an act of faith that life is dictated by something other than numbers, and part of that faith for the players is that the dealer will be lucky for them. There's the story of the player who sat down at a blackjack table and said, "Sure hope I can break even. I need the money." Two sentences, one complete story.

1

BREAKING IN

Before they can make the cards perform ballet in the air, before they can spin a roulette ball at speeds approaching the sound barrier, before they can pay twelve bets on a layout faster than a car salesman can calculate his commission, dealers must learn the basics of the craft. They must *break in* and are therefore called "break-ins." Although it's their hope that their careers will lead them someday to work at the Mirage or Caesars Palace, dealers don't start there; they begin as break-ins at places like the Four Queens or the Horseshoe if they're fortunate or, if not, at the Lady Luck or El Cortez. Before Little Caesar's and Big Wheel were closed and torn town, they were the worst of the break-in joints, dives that offered fifty-cent blackjack and twenty-five-cent craps, heated arguments flying as soon as the dice were tossed, claims about every other hand in blackjack. These were the places where dealers found work on the way up or the way down—the toughest of the tough joints, one-room casinos that bored holes in dealers' eyes and left scars on their souls.

At Little Caesar's, pay was minimum wage and roughly a dollar a day in tips. Across the Strip at the Dunes, craps dealers were knocking down $60,000 a year in tips and keeping most of their wages as well. On her second week of employment at Little Caesar's, a break-in who was feeding her kids with food stamps asked if she should declare income tax on her tips. Sure, the boss told her, put your pennies in a piggy bank. Insane as it may sound, in the early 1980s many dealers were audited and hounded to pay taxes on undeclared tips at places like Little Caesar's, while those who worked at the Dunes or the Sands were granted amnesty if they complied thereafter by declaring the full amount earned to the IRS.

Breaking in is not so much a process of gaining mechanical skills as it is an acclimation, a slow hardening of the soul. Stories of breaking in, although unique taken one at a time, are at the core essentially similar because they evolve from interaction peculiar to casinos where a sprinkling of neon dust and a touch of big-shot treatment turns Goob Wellbody from Sault Sainte Marie into a Bela Lugosi or Lon Chaney caricature.

Dealers survive the daily rigors by recognizing signs, by wearing wreaths of emotional garlic to fend off faux vampires from the Upper Peninsula. Dealers who often have no sense of themselves or their spouses or children often express surprising insights into the forces that operate around them. Cynicism is pervasive. Survival in a casino depends on acquiring it.

A casino is itself a microcosm of a society that desires immediate gratification, risk without danger, reward without labor, recognition without earned respect. Our culture demands a Las Vegas or a Reno or an Atlantic City or the dozens of river-boat casinos found in the South and Midwest to provide an arena in which to act out what is otherwise leashed. We need a place absent of reproach or reprisal. Dealers are sometimes the target of the most outlandish behavior. It is then that they are drawn into the theater, then that they become actors in the comedy or drama. What dealer doesn't have a story?

Dealers merely help facilitate chance but are perceived quite differently. Veterans of the casino wars understand this and have developed mechanisms to deal with it—unflinching eyes, a deadpan expression, methodical motions that express disgust or boredom. But the break-in hasn't developed those skills, just as he or she hasn't acquired the confidence to send a roulette ball whining around the track or the mental facility to count cards on the turn or the dexterity to flip the dice over to the winning point before sending them to the shooter.

Rendering a break-in's story seems merely a matter of transposing names, places, and times; the events will vary in degree, but the gist of their stories is strikingly similar. Old-timers speak of pitbosses kicking them in the ankles and asking almost accusingly, "Can't you win a hand?" Others tell stories of bosses sprinkling salt on losing tables. Both versions suggest, in some way, that when Pascal's mathematics collide with the human desire to control an outcome, superstition and intimidation win. At Little Caesar's, a defunct casino legendary as hell for break-ins, one of the bosses would switch dealers every hand if a player had a streak. At the Mint, a floorman changed decks four times in ten minutes. At the Maxim, a pitboss in craps often took dice off the game to spin and mic them, then he would hide them in his pocket. Men in three-hundred-dollar silk suits have not advanced much beyond the aboriginal stage of the tribesman in New Guinea who paints his face to control the weather. Don't look for calm reasoning here. There are spirits at work.

You're a break-in, and you don't yet have the stories in place, so you try to function on a rational level in an arena where reason is out of place. This is how it begins: confusion, anger, anxiety. Turn the dice over; give the deck an extra shuffle; go slow; go fast; get 'em in the air; dummy up and deal.

1977

You're breaking in at Little Caesar's on graveyard shift. Nothing much happens between 5:00 and 7:00 A.M. One night you're watching a woman named Thelma, also a break-in, as she deals out of a four-deck shoe. You're a minimum-wage dealer who barely knows what to watch for, but it doesn't matter because the pitboss is busy watching action on the craps table, and the blackjack game has just this one player who never bets more than two dollars. Thelma deals a card each to herself and the player, but in the act of turning over the second card to the player, she bows her head, closes her eyes, and the hand with the card stops in midmotion. She stands suspended in that position like a statue in a wax museum.

At first you're stunned, as is the player. Thelma's head nods. Her breathing is shallow, barely audible. You ask if she's okay. But she stands silent, like a machine whose cogs are frozen, a backhoe with its cables snapped. You repeat her name gently, just as you might a sleepwalker's, "Thelma, *Thelma!*" Nothing. You nudge her. Her eyes open, half-lidded, half-comprehending, but dull as blackout drapes. She blinks and lays the card down as if nothing had happened. A sleep disorder, narcolepsy, you think, especially after it happens twice more.

Later, when the craps game dies off, the pitboss wises you up, says Thelma will never make it because she's a junkie. He explains how the casino saves money letting her break in because the state foots the bill. Before coming to Little Caesar's she wrenched her back working as a maid. Now workers' compensation pays the casino to retrain her. She's free labor. You glance over at a dead game where Thelma sits, her eyes closed, head bobbing up and down as if in agreement with everything you've just heard.

"Where else?" the boss says, his voice full of irony.

The irony isn't that the state pays the casino to train a junkie who'll never find regular employment because she's an addict, but rather that the casino pays you minimum wage to watch her and calls it a money-saving arrangement. There's a bigger irony still, and it isn't that the circumstances are ironic, but that no one besides you sees it.

UNDATED

This may be just an urban legend because it has been repeated so many times, gone through so much revision that the source is lost, except that those who have dealt don't doubt it one bit. The story goes that a young female break-in was placed on a blackjack game where a high roller was playing five hundred dollars on five spots. The high roller was way ahead of the game, up more than twenty thousand. This particular woman was picked to go in and deal to him because she had been winning on another game, and the bosses were superstitious. Break-ins, after all, are lucky.

The shift boss and pitboss and floorman hovered nearby. Although nervous, she picked up the deck, shuffled, and offered the cut card to the player, who carefully cut the deck. Hands trembling, she buried the top card and dealt, two cards each to all five of his hands and two for herself. Her top card was an ace. She called for insurance. The pitboss smiled at the shift boss. The axiom about break-ins being lucky was holding up.

One by one the player peeked under each of his hands, pinned the cards under the bets, and when he'd looked at and pinned the last hand, he shook his head, signaling no insurance. The dealer carefully looked at her hole card. She didn't have a face card. She asked if the player wanted a hit. The high roller shook his head. He was good on all hands. She turned over her hole card and hit and hit again to sixteen, then again to an eighteen. The pitboss growled under his breath. The dealer reached to turn over the first of the high roller's hands, but before she could, he swept all of the cards from all of his hands into one pile.

Immediately the pitboss and shift boss charged the table, shouting that he couldn't do that. The player smiled and said, "Just go ahead and pay them."

The boss turned over the cards. The player had ten of the sixteen face cards in the deck. No matter how the hands were arranged he'd have twenty on each of them.

1972

I look back on how audacious I was the first time I tried out for a dealing job. A friend of mine knew Benny Binion, the owner, and had promised he could get me an audition at the Horseshoe. I got a deck of cards, a layout, and some used roulette chips and practiced for two days. Actually a couple of hours each day. On the third night I called my friend. He walked me up to the old man's booth in the front of the restaurant and introduced us. Benny, who was eating a bowl of his famous chili, tilted his hat back and looked me up and down. He seemed a bit amused as he asked how long I'd been practicing. I told him several days.

"You nervous?" he asked.

"No, Sir."

"Then it must be your hands is nervous," he said with a wry smile.

He told me to follow him into the pit. There he introduced me to the pitboss, who pointed to a game. The boss told the dealer on the game that I was coming in for an audition. I tapped the dealer out. The old man stationed himself at the pit podium, that same smile on his lips. I shuffled the cards, which was difficult because the dealer I'd taken out had obviously had honey or glue on his hands. I let one of the players cut the cards and buried the top one. The deck was by then just about the size of a good shipping crate and weighed between nine and ten pounds; still I managed to pitch two cards to each player. The only problem was that I forgot to deal myself a first card. One of the players looked at me as I took the last card and tried to put it under a top that was nonexistent.

"What'cho gonna play with?" the player asked.

The pitboss came over, apologized to the players, and told me to take the first card off the deck and use it as my up card. It was a face card. Now I had to look underneath it to see if I had an ace in the hole. This was no easy task because the deck had nearly doubled in size in the last two seconds. I managed somehow to peek underneath. By then sweat was trickling down my neck, and my armpits were soaked. I went from left to right to give hits to whichever players needed them. Everything went well until I reached the player on third base. He scratched his cards along the felt to ask for a hit. He got more than he expected. The top card was one of the four that landed right in front of his bet. The next thing I knew the pitboss was telling me to pay everyone at the table.

Benny's smile hadn't faded one little bit. He waited for me as I backed away from the table. He tilted his hat back again and said, "Some fellas don't pick this up on the first try. You're welcome to come back sometime and give it your best." Recommending his chili, of course, he told me to have a bite to eat in his restaurant and not to worry about the bill.

Over the years after that I heard a lot of things about Benny Binion and the Horseshoe. I even read about him in *The Green Felt Jungle*. I'll tell you one thing. He was gentleman. I worked for some hard bosses, men and women who did everything they could to bust your chops. I never worked for Benny, but he was a real gentleman. I've told this story to anyone who wanted to hear a Binion story. A real gentleman.

1978

A dealer tells of a New Year's Eve shift at the Mint, where he broke in. On his first break of the shift he walked across the street to the Golden Nugget and downed a shot of brandy. On his second he went to the Horseshoe and did the same. It was New Year's Eve, and he was working his ass off, a twelve-hour shift—his second in two days—already seven straight hours of standing and dealing blackjack and five more hours facing him. The air was oppressive with heat from humans packed together like stockyard animals, and looking out through the smoky casino was like peering inside a house through a screen door. At the craps tables people were shouting like holy rollers in the clasp of the ghost. Ike dollars clattered in slot trays. The slots rang. These sounds along with the steady hum of human noise pounded in his ears. In the lounge a band named Cidro's Armada played "Desperado" to a packed room. The song jolted something inside the dealer. It spoke to him of desperation, the fences he was riding. Too many hands, too many fences. Nobody caring. But a cowboy could turn his life into poetry. A dealer needed a lot of fantasy and a shot of brandy, and still his only poetry came out doggerel.

On his third break the dealer walked around the block with two others. They passed a joint back and forth, some "righteous" Colombian red. They laughed and watched the pale smoke and the vapors from their breath dissolve in the dry cold air. They looked up at the dome of light overhead and at the twinkling neon street behind. It was escape, rebellion. The dealer felt like a desperado, imagined the solitude of riding fences on a cold winter night, imagined leather chaps flapping against a leather saddle and the smell of leather and sage and dust. He got high, so high that he was smiling mindlessly when he returned to the game. His feet no longer hurt, and the slots sounded like tinkling chimes. This time another band, Winchester Cathedral, was on stage. The music was generic and lifeless. He dealt out the first hand and suddenly felt emptied, as if a claw had reached inside him and pulled his heart out.

Where was the Desperado? He began to think of the Desperado as a real person, as his alter ego. The pitboss came up behind him and told him to keep the cards in the air and see if he could win an occasional hand. Wouldn't a real desperado react? Throw the cards in the air? Do something bold and defiant?

His fourth break came at 11:15. He dashed outside, pushed through the crowd at the Golden Nugget, and grabbed another brandy in time to swallow it and make it back to his table. Cidro's Armada was playing again. The band would finish with the song "Desperado." As he waited, he passed time thinking of some character like the Marlboro Man, some lonely soul riding against a mythic landscape. To hell with this, he thought. It's New Year's for everyone else, but a desperado wouldn't care. He delivered cards to the players mechanically, without conversation. After all, talking to players was discouraged. His head was buzzing.

Just before midnight the band played "Desperado." He was waiting for it. It was magical. He stopped his shuffle long enough to look at the stage. The electric guitars glistened in the white spotlight. The pitboss bumped him in the back and said, "You aren't paid to watch."

Perhaps it was the memory of "Desperado." Or was it "Auld Lang Syne"? Or the countdown and the crowd noise? Maybe the booze or marijuana? Or a combination of two drugs? Maybe it was all of them. But he doesn't think so as he tells the story. He says it was the pitboss in his ear, busting his chops near the end of a twelve-hour shift, his sore feet, his back knotted from pain, and the thought of what a desperado might do. At midnight he paid every bet on the table although he'd hit to twenty-one, paid them intentionally, and smiled as he cut into their bets. It was the one time in his life he'd done anything dishonest, something outrageous. It is the one moment he best remembers in twenty years of dealing.

1975

The first night that she goes on a live game to practice, a player leans forward and looks directly at her breasts. He asks if she's hiding any cards in there. Don't cry, she thinks, whatever else don't let him have the satisfaction of seeing you break down. When she doesn't answer, he calls her a bitch. She will be soon enough.

If you can't take it, get out, she's been told. The man wants her to fail. She looks about. Mostly men. She thinks of herself as a pioneer because only a handful of women are dealing on the Strip at the time she's breaking in. One day it will be different; she will look about and see mostly women, and dealing will be just a job and a financial prison for her, and she will have claws in her tongue and steel around her emotions, but on this night she tells herself that everything will be fine if she can just get a job on the Strip. Her stomach rises up, and she swallows it each time she approaches a table. It's the eyes looking at her, saying to her, you're a woman, you're open season.

The same player slides a twenty-five-dollar check into his square. "Bet you're a real bitch," he says.

Her cheeks burn. She buries the first card and says, "Good luck, Sir," while under her breath she mutters, "Asshole."

In time she discovers that male dealers are similarly degraded, that no one behind a game is immune to this. The insults remain. The compensation for taking them just increases.

By the end of the week she's gained this much insight: Slave owners were cruel because nothing stopped them from being cruel. She knows that if she wants the job, there's a price to pay—insults, dehumanizing comments. The player betting the money is all powerful; the dealer is helpless. How do people become machines? How do women become bitches?

Three years later she's at Caesars Palace, where dealers earn in the neighborhood of $60,000 a year. On her first night she's assigned to a one-hundred-dollar-minimum game. All goes well until past 2:00 A.M., when a high roller hands her a three-hundred-dollar toke. He asks how much she charges for sex. She winks and says she doesn't charge her husband anything. The player laughs and tosses her another hundred. She has almost forgotten that first night three years earlier—almost.

1978

The boss calls him over as he's leaving a game. In a friendly manner and kindly tone of voice the boss asks the break-in to do him a favor. It seems that the roulette wheel heads are slowing down and the nearest wheel crank is at the Horseshoe. Would you go get it, he asks. The young dealer, fresh out of dealer's school and anxious to impress so he can make the extra board, eagerly says yes. A good word can speed the hiring process. The boss adds that the dealer should not come back without the crank.

At the Horseshoe the pitboss is extremely friendly and picks up the phone immediately. He tells the break-in to be patient and calls around because they haven't had the wheel crank for two days now. He talks on the telephone, all the while smiling at the young dealer-to-be. When he hangs up the receiver, he tells the young man to go to the Union Plaza, that the wheel crank was last sent there.

The pitboss in the Union Plaza is enthusiastic. He understands how hard it is to track the wheel crank down because some casinos forget where it last went, and no one ever bothers to return it. As did the boss at the Horseshoe, this one makes a quick phone call, smiling at the break-in over the receiver in a friendly way. He hangs up. Although it can't be verified, the crank, he's sure, was last in the possession of the Four Queens. The break-in sets out to find it there.

Over the next three hours, the break-in visits every casino on Fremont Street and is never sent to an adjacent business. It's always two blocks or more, up and back. He doesn't chase down a wheel crank, but he's afraid to return empty handed. He sits in the lounge of the El Cortez and vacillates between calling and explaining he's still looking for the elusive crank and just returning to the casino and admitting failure. The boss seemed to have so much faith in him. He figures it might delay his being hired in either case, so he goes back to where he started from.

The boss looks at him for a moment as if mystified, then he nods. In fact, he's forgotten that he sent the break-in after the phantom wheel crank. He smiles and tells the young man he should have come back sooner, that he was absent when the schedule was made and new hires were added. The break-in asks if something can't be done. No, the pitboss would like to help, but no. He tells the break-in to go to the help's hall and eat.

It is only after he's finished with his cheeseburger and is telling the story to a regular dealer that he finds out how roulette wheels are designed and balanced to run on centrifugal force, that there is no wheel crank, never has been one, that it was all a joke and that everyone was in on it. The pitboss laughs when he sees the break-in walk into the blackjack pit, not a mean laugh but a knowing one. He tells the break-in to get a good sleep and come in the next night ready to go on the payroll. He says he's been hired on the steady extra board.

1980

I was in my third year downtown, way beyond the break-in stage, working the floor once or twice a week. One night it was slow at the Mint, and I got an early out along with a couple of my girlfriends. In order to unwind, we went to the Horseshoe, where I could get a few free drink coupons from a boss who was a friend of mine. We had a bad night, very little in tokes, hardly enough for a day's food, and decided to make a lay-down on the blackjack game, try and turn the tokes into something better. If we didn't, it was no big deal. I was doing okay when along came this Asian woman to audition for a job. She was wearing black-and-whites, with her blouse unbuttoned so that enough of her showed to keep a boss interested. She tapped out the regular dealer and picked up the deck off the layout. None of this made me very happy because I was well ahead of the game.

It was pretty obvious she didn't have much experience because she could barely shuffle the cards. She made it around the table okay the first couple of rounds, but her hands were shaking something terrible. Usually after about four or five hands a dealer who's auditioning for a job will settle down, and her dealing will get smoother and cleaner. It didn't happen in this lady's case. We were winning, and it soon became apparent to me that she resented our winning. Maybe she thought her getting the job depended on our losing. The boss just watched her, occasionally smiling as he did.

About twenty minutes into her audition she dealt a blackjack to this guy on the game who happened to be the only big bettor. Her face was red as she reached over and paid him off. She snatched up his cards, but instead of placing them in the discard rack, she folded the cards, lifted the paddle on the drop box, and shoved the cards in where the money goes. I lost it when the boss came over and asked where she'd learned to do that.

1983

I was on the floor on graveyard at the Maxim, which wasn't a break-in joint. Most of the dealers were required to have three years' experience to work there. In those days it was a good house in terms of tips. The casino manager was known to be kind of his own person, which is another way of saying he had some unorthodox notions, but he'd also do some very humane things from time to time. One of his little acts of kindness came after a porter found a wallet with several hundred dollars in it. The porter turned the wallet in, and the casino manager took this act of honesty to heart and gave the porter a job as a dealer.

At the time, we got some pretty good action in the casino, especially on late swing shift and early graveyard. Well, the porter was assigned to graveyard. That meant he came in at four o'clock in the morning. At the same time another of the casino manager's project dealers (people who he was determined would become dealers), a woman who'd worked in the accounts department as a secretary, was also breaking in. I spent half my time watching these two break-ins and correcting their mistakes.

By the end of the first month the ex-porter still couldn't pay off a blackjack, any blackjack other than a two-dollar bet, without making a mistake. Every blackjack payout, no matter how many times he'd made the payoff before, flustered him as much as the last one had, and yet every time I came to his aid he got upset and even more nervous. More than once I thought the poor guy was going to have a seizure.

The woman, on the other hand, made mistakes because she tried to go too fast and carry on conversations with the players, and it was impossible to correct her mistakes without her whining about being corrected and reminding me how she had her job because the casino manager wanted her to have it because she was "so good with people." When she looked at her hole card, players in the MGM across the street could see it. Of the two, she was the harder to supervise. The ex-porter, essentially a nice guy, was thankful for getting a dealer's job, and he tried but just wasn't competent.

Invariably, the two of them ended up in my pit.

One morning I was exhausted already from watching the two of them and correcting their mistakes when I finally got a well-earned but short break. Earl, the floorman who relieved me, had been in the business for more than twenty-five years. He always looked like he'd been interrupted from a nap, but he knew the score. He told me to take a fifteen. He looked at the ex-porter and the ex-secretary and said, "Well, well, Lumpville. Have a good break and hurry back."

When I returned the ex-porter was staring at a player's fifteen-dollar bet and trying to figure out what to pay the player for his blackjack. He took a stack of five-dollar chips out of the rack and set them before him on the layout but didn't do anything with them, just stared at the black-jack. A couple of seconds later he put those back in the rack and scratched his head. Now he came out with a stack of twenty-five-dollar checks. He scratched his head again. It was obvious that he had advanced beyond flustered to completely boggled. He scraped the toe of his shoe over the carpet. I asked Earl if he was going to help the dealer.

Earl looked at me with his perpetually drowsy-eyed look and said, "When he scratches his ass, I'll go over."

It wasn't half a second later that the ex-porter reached behind himself and scratched his butt.

"Excuse me," Earl said. "Time to go help."

1977

It's early in the graveyard shift, and the dealer has been running hot now for thirty minutes. The cab driver, out two hundred dollars, is steaming. He mumbles under his breath. This is Little Caesar's across from the Dunes. It's a dive—or worse, if you listen to the people who work there—supervised by has-been pitbosses who can't get a decent job and manned by break-in dealers who want to gain enough experience and skill to audition for a better-paying one. Mostly the customers are cabbies or degenerates, and sometimes one and the same.

One night, so the story went, a man came in and said he was there to remodel. He stretched a strip of metallic duct tape over a tear in the rug, pressed it down, and stepped on it. Bingo! Remodeling complete, he left.

Cabbies get drunk here and lose their money. The joint's owned by a man who also owns two cab companies. He sees nothing ironic in cashing his cab drivers' checks and taking their money in his casino. It's business. But sometimes the cab drivers get down too far; some get buried. This one is down to his last three dollars. He stands, takes two steps back, calls the dealer a string of four-letter names, and heaves three Eisenhower dollars, hitting the break-in's chest.

Under normal conditions in any other casino, a security guard would throw the offender out of the place. But this, as has been stated, is Little Caesar's. Here it's a good shift if no one vomits on the table. Here, there are no guards. The prevailing rule is somewhat akin to the law of the wild, the code of the West, the order of Darwinian survival. Under other circumstances the cab driver might also have gotten by with his misdeed. But again, this is Little Caesar's, and the pay is minimum wage, and tips run somewhere in the neighborhood of $1.75 per day, not a wage worth worrying about, not a job with a future. In the best-case scenario the cabby would have tossed those coins at a 130-pound coward or a woman of equal size. But this, once again, is Little Caesar's, and the dealer is a thirty-year-old ex-cop who weighs 190 pounds and who's tired of being called four-letter names and who doesn't care much for the likes of cab drivers who blow their paychecks on blackjack games and, most importantly, who doesn't care if he loses his job. That's how the footrace begins.

The chase ends at Churchill Downs Sports Book, which happens to be closed at 4:00 A.M. The cab driver runs out of foul language and space at the same instant. The only four-letter word he now knows is "Help!" No one passing by seems to understand that word or wants to hear it or dares to intercede while the ex-cop, new break-in throws punches at the cowering cabby. It's over in three minutes. The break-in, his rage spent, looks down at the cabby, who's bleeding from the nose and sporting a large mouse on his left eye.

"Got something else to say?" he asks.

The cab driver says nothing.

Back in Little Caesar's the pitboss stands beside the blackjack game while another dealer straightens the bank. The pitboss wants to know what happened. The break-in says "not much" and asks where the three Eisenhower dollars are. The boss says he locked them up in the rack. Shaking his head, the break-in insists that the money is his, a tip, he says. This is Little Caesar's, where tips are a pittance and every dollar helps.

Two nights later the cabby returns, sits down at the blackjack game, and buys in for forty dollars. It's Little Caesar's. Where else can he play for fifty cents a hand if things go bad? The dealer shakes his head and calls out, "Change forty!"

1978

At twenty-six, she has two kids—a girl five and a boy three—and a mortgage, responsibilities. She's still on the extra board after eight months and working only three or four days a week, making barely enough to make the house payment and feed her kids. She seeks the advice of another dealer, a woman a year or two older, who's been in the business three years. They sit on the couch in the break room, smoking and talking. The younger one talks around the subject, says that her ex-husband isn't real good about child support, that she's been late twice with the mortgage.

The older woman listens, occasionally sucking on a cigarette and blowing the smoke at the ceiling. She's a good listener and quickly figures out in what direction the conversation's headed. Before it gets too intimate for her liking, she snuffs out her cigarette.

"Tell you what," she says and names the man who schedules the dealers. "He's the guy to see."

The younger dealer says the man intimidates her. The older one understands because he used to intimidate her as well. She smiles knowingly and looks the other up and down. "He's a man. You're attractive. Figure it out." The older one stands and smooths her skirt, checks her nylons in the mirror, and starts to leave. She has a second thought. "I'll tell him you have a problem. That way he'll make the approach. Never know, you could get to like him."

1985

She stands squarely in front of the rack and listens to the boss who's telling her his personal problems. He's got a few: child support and a car payment, two credit cards run up to the limit. He adds that his cat is pregnant, then quickly says he's not the father. The dealer laughs. She likes the attention. She's twenty-four and slender and, with the right touch of makeup, attractive, no beauty, but the kind who doesn't have to worry about being ignored.

She wonders why he's picked her to talk to. True, it's slow. She tells him about her boyfriend's new car just to let him know she's with someone. He says he wanted a Cougar himself, but the damned child support is four hundred a month. A customer sits down, and she shuffles the deck. The boss tells her to see him when she gets off the game.

He says he's been watching her for a while now, and if she's not real involved with this boyfriend, maybe the two of them could get together for a drink. He's very soft spoken and apologetic and interested but noncommittal, as if stuck in neutral with the engine racing. She thinks of her boyfriend and how long they've been going together, two years and everything is stalled. But some of the time they have fun, when they can manage to get together. He works as a mechanic, daytime work, and she's working swing shift. It's hard to get together. On his days off, he wakes her up before noon or earlier if they have decided to go someplace. She's always too tired to enjoy it. He likes movies or a drive to the mountains. He's very safe, but lately they don't seem to have anything in common. He doesn't understand what she's talking about when she discusses her work any more than she knows how to change a pressure plate. He's not interested in marriage, not now. He already has one family, one busted marriage, but he wouldn't mind "setting up house," if she had a day job.

"Why don't you be a secretary?" he asked.

It's always that or a bank teller. What does a secretary make? she thought. Nothing.

If all goes well for her, in two years she'll be dealing on the Strip making four or five times what a secretary is paid. This is on her mind as her relief dealer taps her on the shoulder.

The boss tells her to go take her break. Think about it, but don't take offense. She's not offended, in fact, is a little flattered. For the duration of the break she thinks about her conversation with the boss. Why not? He's older, maybe even forty, but attractive, a good dresser. Smooth, maybe too smooth. She likes his confidence. She remembers how he scared her when he first watched her deal and nitpicked at her and made her feel clumsy and small. "Lobster claws" he called her. Well, that was then.

As she passes him she says nothing, just smiles in a friendly way. He follows her to the table and stands close behind, so close that she can feel his body heat fill the space. But he doesn't touch her. The players place their bets, and she deals to them. The boss's mouth is so close to her ear that she feels a tingling down her legs. It is then that she looks down and sees that she's given the players two cards each but none to herself.

She's humiliated to tell the boss what she's done. He merely tells her to pick up the cards and deal a new hand as he explains politely to the customers that it was a simple mistake, that the dealer is new and means well. He whispers that they should meet after work at the Brewery, a disco on Paradise Road. His hand brushes down her back. She nods because it is the only way that she can deal the next hand. As soon as she agrees to meet him she feels relieved, not happy but relieved. She knows it's wrong, but others do it. Besides, he'll understand what she's talking about.

1977

He arrived to audition for a craps job at the Mint but was told there were no openings except in blackjack. How hard can it be to deal blackjack? He needed a job *that* day, so he said he could deal blackjack. The casino manager marched him down to the pit and told the pitboss to put the break-in on a game to audition.

"How long you been dealing?" the boss asked. He chewed gum. Several sticks at once, by the look of it.

"Three months," the break-in said, which was a lie. He'd dealt just one month, and only craps, never blackjack.

"Go in there," the boss said, pointing at a female dealer.

The break-in tapped out the woman, who seemed happy to get the unexpected break. She was about thirty but seemed much older in the eyes when she backed away. She stood to his left to watch as he buried the first card. Four players sat on the game. He looked each one in the face and smiled before he turned over the first card. He wanted them on his side. The last player he looked at was a man on third base who was wearing a soiled red and black plaid shirt. He smelled badly of body odor and liquor. He looked down at the layout and didn't return eye contact.

As the break-in slid the top card out of the shoe and delivered it rather awkwardly to the first player, the woman dealer leaned toward the table and told him to deal slowly and not be nervous. She smiled to encourage him. He nodded and turned over the next card to the second player and so forth. As he was dealing the second set of cards, he glimpsed movement to his right, a red sleeve. In the corner of his eye he saw the man's hand reaching toward the discard rack where the dealer had stacked chips given her as tips. The woman's view of that part of the layout was blocked, and the pitboss had turned away from the game. When the hand grabbed the chips, the break-in clamped his hand over the man's and squeezed.

The man released a sharp whine.

They struggled, the man trying to pull free, the break-in clamping down tighter and tighter and twisting the man's wrist back. The woman dealer was confused until one of the other players shouted that the man on third base was trying to steal her tokes.

"I thought they were mine," the man protested.

The pitboss wheeled about and, seeing the tug-of-war, hurried over.

"Let go of me!" the man shouted.

Heads turned at the nearby tables.

All the while the break-in had said nothing. Now, thinking that he'd lost the job, he turned to the pitboss and said, "Don't know what to do."

"Goddamnit, let go a' me," the man said.

The boss smiled and placed his open palm under the man's hand. "You can let go," he said to the break-in.

The pitboss told the man to put the chips back, picked up the two cards in front of his square, and told him to leave or be arrested. Mumbling, the man backed away from the table and when he was at a safe distance said that he was going to sue, then turned and ran.

"Finish the hand," the boss said.

As the break-in finished the hand and put the cards in the discard rack, the dealer tapped him out and told him to report to the pitboss.

"I only dealt one hand," he said to the pitboss.

The boss looked at him dispassionately. "Uh-huh."

"I didn't mean to cause a scene," the break-in said.

The pitboss looked him up and down, then nodded as if in disgust. "Go back to the casino manager's office. His secretary will give you some papers to fill out."

"I got the job?"

The boss looked at the overhead mirrors that reflected the games up and down the pit. He studied the action on one of the layouts and said without looking at the break-in, "If you want to get along with me, just do what you're told."

1971

Every question that a break-in asks is stupid, unless it's about where to eat. At least that's what one boss told me. What you learn to do is nod as if you understand, even if you haven't the foggiest, and figure it out for yourself later. Know what I mean? They tell you something, you nod. That's how it is.

I was breaking in on craps. It was my third night, and the boss comes up behind me as I'm about to clap out.

"Take the silver to the toke box when you clap out," he said.

What he meant was to exchange any dollar chips I had gotten as tokes for metal dollar tokens. We don't deal the metal ones on craps. They slide, you see. So, anyhow, this boss gave me the order. But I didn't know what he meant. I thought he meant for me to take the metal ones as tips and drop them, so I did—every night for almost a month. How many I dropped I have no idea. Then one night one of the other bosses stopped me and asked what the hell I thought I was doing. I gave him the honest answer. He asked where the hell I'd gotten that idea into my head. I told him what the other boss had said. Well, everyone got such a big laugh out of it that I wasn't fired. Stupid break-in, they said, stupid break-in.

1982

There was this guy downtown who used to beg out of a wheelchair. He'd sit out in front of the Four Queens with his cup until it was full of quarters and nickels, then he'd roll himself inside and find the nearest slot machine to play, taking coins right out of his cup and dropping them in the coin slot.

1982

Tyrone was famous downtown. He wore roller skates wherever he went, up and down Fremont Street, in and out of casinos. The guards at the Nugget grabbed him one night and told him not to come in again in skates. Well, Tyrone was a Korean War vet and not quite right in the head, so he simply turned it into a game. He'd come in the door and catch the eye of a guard and take off. The chase was on. I heard they'd caught him once and worked him over. I don't know about that because it didn't seem to slow him down one little bit.

One night I was standing near the door to the parking lot looking up at the sky when Tyrone stopped beside me. He looked up and asked what I was looking at. I told him the stars. He stood there staring with me for a second and said they were coming after him. I asked who? The guards? He pointed up to the sky. "Them," he said.

I went to work on the Strip a year or so later. I saw a lot of strange, even interesting people, but no Tyrones. Someone told me he died. I like to think that "they" came for him.

2

MATTRESS POLITICS

As in any environment where the sexes mingle, casinos are rife with gender and sexual conflict. Until recently, sexual harassment was commonplace, even expected. It came, as the expression goes, "with the territory." Men in positions of power supervising women thought nothing of approaching them, whether or not they were married or otherwise involved, about "getting together." The notion of "together," of course, meant sex of some sort. The men at the top seemed to figure it was part of the privilege of their position, and in some instances (perhaps many) female dealers invited the behavior.

Part of the problem is that management decisions in casinos are often arbitrary. Another part of the problem is that dealers work at the pleasure of the casino, which means naturally that they work at the pleasure of the decision makers who run the casinos, most usually casino managers, shift bosses, and pitbosses. I would be remiss not to mention other possibilities that encourage sexual involvement between dealers and supervisors, one of which may very well be that the job, the actual task of dealing, is boring, as are many jobs, and that a tryst or contemplating one may be one way of alleviating the boredom. The work is stressful, and any given boss from floor person to casino manager can make the job miserable for the dealer. Bosses decide where a dealer will spend an eight-hour shift, whether on a two-dollar-minimum blackjack game or a roulette table in the high-roller section, as well as what shift and what days off a dealer will have and when that dealer can take a vacation or an extra day off, which means the bosses are in a position to grant favors. Add to all of this the "juice" system, where jobs and favors go to those who are on the bosses' good side, and all the ingredients are there to facilitate a job environment that promotes sexual harassment, gender bias, and privilege.

Although sexual harassment suits against casinos have been filed in recent years, most go nowhere or are settled out of court for a pittance. The exception was the Tailhook scandal, which went to federal court. It was adjudged that the Hilton, which had a commitment to protect both employees and customers from sexual harassment, had failed in its responsibility to intervene when Navy and Marine Corps pilots formed a gauntlet in one of the hotel's hallways and fondled women who made the error of being there at the wrong time. The court felt that the hotel had shirked its responsibility to protect its guests. On the other hand, a suit brought by one of the Hilton's female dealers against the hotel for sexual harassment went to court, and the dealer lost. It seems she had told a customer who was watching her game to "go fuck yourself." Why she did this is a matter of conjecture, but she claimed that in looking at her he was leering and that thus it was sexual harassment and encouraged or, at least, condoned by the casino. Ironically, she was a pretty woman who groomed herself to be as attractive as possible and was naturally noticed by customers.

The Hilton had clearly stated rules that forbade employees using profanity toward customers. The customer complained. Several witnesses backed up his story. Management found no evidence of sexual harassment, so the dealer was fired for violating the rule against addressing foul language at a customer. She sued the Hilton, claiming that the casino management had not protected her from sexual harassment and in fact encouraged such behavior from customers. The case went to court. The dealer lost. (An interesting aside: The dealer who filed the harassment suit had been a prostitute before she became a dealer, which certainly doesn't preclude the possibility that she could be harassed but suggests that she knew full well the measure of what "being attractive" means in terms of eliciting attention.) I mention these facts to show that innocence is not an issue in this particular instance. Before the Tailhook case the Hilton management probably didn't take adequate measures to stem sexual harassment. However, this particular dealer stretched the notion of what constitutes sexual harassment to a degree that insults every woman who has actually been harassed.

Consensual relations and love affairs in casinos far outnumber instances of sexual harassment. Dealers are men and women. Bosses are men and women. Casinos are a microcosm of society, and wherever men and women gather, relationships and affairs will result. Gay relationships are common in casinos as well. But it seems to me that the relationships, the types of affairs, the sex for favors, the favors for sex, the acts of sexual harassment, the play, the games, and the jealousies that transpire in casinos are somehow unique. Perhaps it's the public nature of the casino pit or the close quarters in which casino employees work, or perhaps it's the stress or the cynical attitudes of dealers and their high divorce rates, but most love and sex relationships in casinos seem like parodies of relationships, more desperate and more doomed.

1978

It was one big party that year I spent downtown. A damned orgy. Many, maybe most, of the dealers were single or divorced, working odd hours, sometimes twelve-hour shifts. And all of us were uptight and not too damned rich. To unwind we smoked grass, drank, and played musical playmates. The same dose of crabs went through the casino five or six times while I was there. You could have made a living selling delousing spray.

I was kind of seeing this one woman—I'll call her Mabel—but without a commitment. She was different from most of us. She'd actually graduated from college and then dropped out of law school because it disillusioned her, as if dealing wasn't going to disillusion her more. But what did we know?

One evening I'm eating with Mabel in the help's hall when I look over, and here comes a woman I'd had a fling with about two weeks earlier. She plops down at our table. I decide it's best to shift the conversation to something mundane and keep it there so as to cover my butt. I mention tips and how I got stiffed by a player who'd won a bundle. This topic normally spurs itself—one story following the next, each dealer trying to outdo the last. And I had it going real good, until I look up, and along comes a third woman, one who'd been to my apartment after work the previous shift. She'd been hassling with her boyfriend over him ignoring her. We'd had a few drinks and ended up at my place. Well, she—I'll call her Mary—has got her tray in hand using it like a steering wheel as she maneuvers to our table.

Mary sets her tray next to Mabel's, then before she sits down says, "You'll never guess what George did."

George was the boyfriend she was hassling with.

"What did George do?"

"He gave me the goddamn crabs," she said.

I casually picked at a chicken wing, dropped it on my plate, and excused myself.

I guess I knew as I walked away that it was over between Mabel and me anyhow. Like I said, it was one big party. How we survived it is beyond me. It was a couple of years before AIDS hit the scene. When I look back, that's one of the things I'm thankful for. It's twenty years later, and now Mabel's my boss at the casino I work in, and with three divorces and a fourth one on the cusp, she's about as disillusioned as anyone can get. I may have had something to do with it, but she doesn't remember things the way I do. She thought I was a nice guy back then. She says things might have been better for both of us if we'd gotten married.

Get married? Miss that party? Not on your life. I make pretty good money now. Hell, I make as much as anyone in the trades and more than some professionals do, make a hell of a lot more than the professors I took classes from at the university. But I'm miserable. There's no party out here on the Strip. Work is just a daily grind. I was happier when I was breaking in and making thirty-five a day in tokes; so were Mabel and Mary and George.

1981

I was in my twenties. I won't say how into them, but old enough. I'd broken in downtown, done a year and some months at the Horseshoe, and figured I was ready, so I put out applications for auditions. I must have gone to eight or nine Strip properties, all big ones. There were no megaresorts in those days, and you took what you could get. The big money was Caesars and the Trop. I was hoping for a spot there, but anything would be better than downtown.

I finally hit one place; I won't say where. I was told at personnel to take the application up to the pit and page the casino manager himself. I was really excited. All the other joints had said we'll call you or you keep calling us or come back, always something. But here they hooked me up with an audition right away. I was wearing black-and-whites and neat, hair and nails done, you know, professional as I could considering that I was still green. I was attractive and could deal a decent blackjack game because I'd had to deal to big money at the 'Shoe and kind of knew the wheel, although I wasn't ready for serious action. I figured, and this is still true, a pretty face helps. Let's face it, high rollers like someone to look at when they're blowing money. It's a human world out there. I'm not saying I was every man's fantasy, but I wasn't hard to look at. You get the picture.

So, I page the guy. He says to meet him at the end of the blackjack pit by a bar. I see him as I approach. I stand as tall as I can and walk up real confident, trying to make a solid impression. I don't want him to think I'm intimidated or anything. But I wasn't exactly cocky. He shook my hand and took the application. He looked it over for about ten seconds, then nodded. He held the application behind his back and looked me up and down. I figured he'd tell me to come back or say he wanted me to audition later.

He didn't bat an eye. He looked me square in the eye and said, "Do you fuck?"

I was stunned. What century is this, I thought. Here's this guy too young to be a casino manager and who I find out later never dealt a game in his life, who got juiced in because he was friends with the major stockholder, and he's wearing a six-hundred-dollar silk suit made in Italy, and he's nothing but a pig. I wanted to slap him, and I wanted to cry, but I just stood there shaking and humiliated. He wasn't fazed in the least. He looked at the application, looked at me, and said, "Guess not."

The problem, and it's still a problem, is it's his word against mine, and I was the one looking for a job. Trouble is, some women went for it. It was bad all around, not just for women like me, but for men, too. How can anyone compete fairly for a job if the ground rules are stacked against her? It's still there, that old attitude, but it's subtler now. Besides, at my age no one's all that interested. But I can deal four games now as well as anyone. Next time I went out looking for a job, I got a couple of auditions and was hired because I could deal. Still, I think about what that son of a bitch could get by with and get angry. Who wouldn't?

1987

I'll call her Lisa. This is going back thirteen years. Lisa attracted men without trying, not beautiful, but pretty in a girlish way and vulnerable looking so that you kind of thought she was out of place in a casino. I mean, a lot of guys hit on her—dealers, bosses, players. She didn't stop them, either, which isn't to say she went for them. No, she just played along with them. She liked the attention. We got together about two months after she came to work on my shift. I was in craps, and she was pumping cards, so we didn't trip over each other or any of that stuff that goes on when two people work the same games.

We got a new boss on our shift. He came in from another casino. He was the brassy kind of guy who wanted to reinvent gambling, which has been pretty much the same since those Roman soldiers threw lots for Christ's garments. He made the same kinds of changes everyone tries. No talking to players unless it has to do with the game. Don't light up a cigarette in the casino on the way to the break room. No crossfire on the game. Standard. Of course, in craps you can't make a living if you don't cut into the players. We hustle. We have to in joints where we go for ourselves. Any craps dealer who says otherwise is a bald-faced liar. But we did slow down.

Anyhow, this guy notices Lisa right away. She was the only dealer he introduced himself to that first night. Walks up to her in his six-hundred-dollar Italian suit and two-hundred-dollar shoes and tells her he's been watching her game and thinks she's one hell of a dealer. She lights up. The truth is she'd been dealing about a year and was just another clerk, no speed demon or superstar. Next thing you know, he's sitting on her game when she's got no players, and he's chummy as hell, turning on the charm like Nevada Power Company had charm wires shoved up his rectum and were pouring the juice to him. He took to confiding in her. The hook was how lonely it was at the top and how nice it was that she'd listen to him.

Finally he hits on her. She says she's got a boyfriend but doesn't say who. He finds out anyhow. Soon enough he's watching my game, sometimes from the edge of the podium in the pit, other times from across the casino. Lisa tells me how nice he is, how understanding, and insists that he's not up to anything.

As I said, we'd cooled our action a bit since he'd arrived, but it was getting stressful on the bank accounts. We had married men with families and mortgages on the crew. Bills were due, and we were grinding out under a bill a night. This high roller we knew strolled in from Caesars. He'd had a bad run there and hoped he could put a roll together on our game. He was kind of george, but you had to work him. You know, talk it up, like "How's the wife, Mr. G?" and "Don't forget the odds." Now, one of the new shift boss's rules was no hustling odds. Hustle the flat bets and the proposition bets because they favor the house, but the odds are a dead-even prop. So Mr. G's down on the come for five hundred, and the dice are moving, and the guy on the opposite base who's dealing to Mr. G says, "You didn't take odds on your last come, sir." So Mr. G calls, "One thousand odds on the nine." And the box man calls out "Bet," and marks up the thousand with a lammer.

Bam! Nine hits. Well, the feces strike the propeller. The shift boss lands next to the game like he was parachuted in, wanting to know this and that from the floorman. Now, keep in mind that when we made a score, every boss in the pit, the box man, the floormen, the pitboss got a layoff. Hell, we bought a few cars for them over the years with the envelopes they got, and they didn't pay a penny of tax on any of it. The floorman said he heard the call, and the box man confirmed it. That's really all that was needed in the way of explanation. But not tonight. Near the end of the shift we close down the game a half-hour early. We'd made a score. Mr. G caught a couple of good hands and walked with about eighty grand. We cut up about two grand a man before layoffs, which would be handed out when we met the bosses in the parking lot after work. We decide to give an extra layoff to the floorman who'd covered for us.

The shift boss comes into the pit and says he wants to talk to each of us individually, says he has some questions. He doesn't have any questions, just accusations. In so many words, he told each of us that he knew we were stealing from the joint, that hustling and stealing were both the same to him. Mind you, this guy had been a craps dealer at the

Tropicana and the Dunes in the old days when they hustled using everything but revolvers. He'd been what was known in the business as a hard hustler.

I got out of there about an hour before Lisa could. We were supposed to meet at my place, but she didn't show. A while later I got a call from her. She's upset. She says rumor is that my crew has been caught cheating, and the gaming control board is going to be called in. I tell her that is absurd. She doesn't come over.

Next night, she passes by my game as she comes into the pit to sign in. My game's dead. She says she wants to talk to me in private and asks what break I'm on. We meet that next break. She says the shift boss confided in her that I was in trouble but that I can save my job if I tell on who hustled Mr. G for the odds bet. I tell her our new boss is full of it, that he is seeing ghosts and goblins. She says that she hopes I'm right.

It was slow that shift. I looked up on a couple of occasions and saw the shift boss seated at Lisa's game. That night she came over to my place. I popped a cork, and we lit the fireplace. It was only gas but romantic enough for what I had in mind. She wanted to talk. She told me how the new boss was going to forget about that incident with Mr. G, but, of course, he'd be keeping a tight eye on us.

A week went by, and in the middle of a shift the same boss came over and told us to bring up the lid on the game, said that he was going to send us home. He did. He suspended two of the dealers for a week for hustling, gave a warning slip to another for not reporting an infraction, and fired me for looking away from the game. He said I'd been casino gazing, and he'd seen me doing it more than a dozen times, that my concern shouldn't be with my girlfriend but with the game.

To make a long story short, he told Lisa that the real reason I was fired was that I'd been caught stealing and that he was only doing me a favor by firing me. I told her that was a bunch of garbage. Two days later I'd lost my girlfriend. She started seeing him. He was married. I found another job. I'm a good craps dealer. I hustle, and I still hand out layoffs in the parking lot after work, but, hell, you gotta live. I bumped into Lisa a couple of times since then. She married once and has since divorced. She's still kind of pretty but in a hard way. He dumped her about two years after he fired me, divorced his wife, married a dealer young enough to be his daughter, and started a second family. Nothing's changed. The suits still have power, and they use it to get their way. I'm almost fifty and never been married, haven't been sweet on anyone since Lisa. Guess you could say she broke my heart. Probably broke a few others as well. She didn't start out to, just couldn't help it. That's the business.

1977-78

It was like an experiment, men and women working the same jobs, making the same money, most of them free of ties. When the Plaza opened up in 1972, the pit was filled with women dealers. It wasn't long before most of the downtown joints featured a few, then you saw fewer and fewer men behind blackjack tables. Female dealers. A few came down from Reno, but the rest came out of dealers' schools or broke in at joints where they'd been waitresses or secretaries or change girls before.

The Mint was a smorgasbord. Women everywhere. Dealers, cocktail waitresses. I was in my early twenties and didn't have a lick of sense and even less control. It wasn't like I was some continental lover, just another dealer. Maybe it was the times, 1977, I think or later. It was before AIDS. I remember once that someone introduced crab lice into the scene. Those little critters went around the pit like an epidemic. I'm serious. You'd see guys and gals behind a game squirming like something had crawled up their legs. There were a lot of jokes and stories and some finger pointing over that.

I was seeing one woman pretty regularly, a dealer, and playing around with two others. One evening I got to work a little early, went up to the employees' dining hall, and after setting a bowl of soup on a tray, I grabbed a seat at a corner table. In walks Tina, the woman I was dating. She spots me, pours herself some coffee, and comes over. A couple of minutes later Sherry, the one I'd been with the previous night, slides a tray off the line, fixes herself a small salad, sees me, and heads over. Not three seconds later Gloria, a dealer I'd slept with the week before, walks our way with a cup of coffee in hand. She takes the fourth and last seat at the table. In theory, Gloria and Sherry know about Tina, but not each other, and Tina doesn't know about either of them.

"How's things?" Gloria asked me.

"Fine," I said.

"Really?" She looked at Sherry, who smiled and looked at Tina, who wasn't smiling.

"There's something we want to ask you," Tina said.

You didn't have to be a genius to figure out that "we" meant something beyond the first person plural and that the "something" they were interested in discussing wasn't nearly so vague as the word might imply. I nodded a couple of times and excused myself. I figured the vacant chair I'd left behind would answer any questions they had in mind. It was cowardly, sure, but I still think of it as a wise move.

I found out a week or so after that incident that Tina had been sleeping around as well. I think, looking back, that she and the others were asserting their freedom. If they could take on a job that had been reserved for men, they could also be liberated in other behaviors. They weren't just breaking barriers, they were demolishing them. Men and women working together, things happen. It's not like that so much now. Maybe I'm older, but I think it's the times. People have gotten used to the idea that women and men can work together without being obligated to climb into bed together every chance they get. Or maybe we're just uptight now.

UNDATED

I admit I've got a thing for men in suits, the more expensive the suit, the more I'm interested. If it helps my situation a little bit, that's okay, too. Everybody has to survive. So what? There's politics, and then there's politics.

1986

I remember when the first boss hit on me, and I turned him down. He said, "What is it? Do you have a boyfriend?" As if that would make all the difference in the world. I told him no. He said, "Then are you some kind of lesbian?" I was scared as hell when he said it. I think he figured that was supposed to nudge me in his direction. But I was scared mostly because I am a lesbian, and his voice was full of disdain when he used the word. Naturally, I denied it. It seemed the safe thing to do. There's a lot of bias out there, and people like me threaten others simply by virtue of being what we are. They can't understand us, especially in the years that gaming made the early transition from that Mob, macho, patriarchal system to accepting women.

Up to a few years ago a lot of bosses treated women dealers like they were concubines. A pretty face or big breasts were more valued than good work habits or a good personality. I don't hide being gay any longer. I've had the same partner for seven years. We love one another. My friends at work know her, and no one makes a big issue out of it now. Surprisingly, the men I work with in the craps pit are more accepting of it than some of the women in the casino. Although I have to admit that the mature women are very supportive. That's how it's gotten to be over the years.

Corporations own the casinos, but mostly men, men from the old school or the in-between school or whatever you want to call it, run them. Women have had a big impact on the business, but there's still the glass ceiling. Some women have broken through, but largely it's men who run the casinos. And most of the women who have gone to the higher levels aren't . . . Well, let's just say lipstick and long nails aren't threatening to the system. Since I've got an eye on such things, I'll admit I'm sensitive to the issue. I want to get out from behind the craps table. I'm in my early forties, got lots of experience, some college, and would like to get a position not as a floor person necessarily, but something with some serious responsibility and a title. But I feel sometimes like I'm back there when that boss was hitting on me, knowing that being different I will be judged one way.

1997

I'm working the floor on graveyard now. I didn't want to go back into the business, having spent fifteen years teaching tennis. One of the drawbacks of all this construction and everything is that tennis courts keep getting ripped out or closed down. Strip property is just too valuable to waste on tennis courts, which produce relatively little income per square foot on the ground compared to casinos and hotels. I had a good situation at the MGM back in the early eighties, but when it burned down, I was out of a job, just like a few thousand others. I taught at the Sands for a while before those courts were torn down, too; anyhow, to make a long story short, as I was establishing myself as a tennis teacher, I worked as a dealer. The last place was the Castaways, which was also torn down. Then I tore my Achilles tendons, one right after the other.

When it became apparent that I had to do something, because opportunities in pro tennis were thinning out and I was getting older, I started a dealing school. That wasn't lucrative enough to keep my nut going, so I did what I least wanted to do and got a job in a casino, not dealing but as a floor person. A guy I used to teach tennis to and later played gave me the job. It pays enough.

There was this good-looking dealer, one of those svelte black women who make great models. She was about twenty-six or -seven and had been in the business a year or so. She wasn't much of a blackjack dealer and didn't care. She was attractive. That was all that mattered. And she knew, too, believe me. So did the assistant shift boss. In no time they became an item, which was fine. Whose business is that anyhow, if it doesn't interfere with the job? But in this case it did. The assistant shift boss got off work an hour earlier than his dealer girlfriend, so he'd arrange for her to get out early as well. We were always stuck short of help because of it, but he expected us to cover the pit. Dealers got locked in and lost breaks because we were one dealer short. We had to close down games.

Well, I confronted him right in front of the shift boss, the guy who'd hired me. The shift boss just sat on a dead game and watched the fireworks. The other boss wanted to dress me down, wanted to suspend me at first, but when he saw that his boss wasn't going to back him, he just wanted to hide. Not long after that the assistant shift boss was fired. Nothing happened to the dealer. She ended up getting a job at Caesars Palace. Good looks.

The gaming business is what it is. You can't ever understand it if you're an outsider. Things that raise eyebrows or offend people in the regular world are commonplace here. I know. I've been in both worlds. Sometimes I think back to my days on the tennis courts. I liked that work. I miss it. I produced a couple of outstanding junior players. The people I taught respected my ability. Here I make a buck, and pretty faces get seventy-thousand-dollar-a-year dealing jobs.

1981

I was on a game the first day Donna was promoted to the floor. She came over as I was bent over the game spreading my deck. She reached down and grabbed one of my cheeks and squeezed. She smiled and said, "They been doing it to me for years. Now it's my turn." What's a guy going to do? File harassment charges?

UNDATED

The worst thing you can do is get involved with a woman dealer if it doesn't work out. I mean, you're son-of-a-bitched in the pit and in the break room by all her friends. They get together and hack away at it. Male bashing is okay. Never mind that the woman may be exaggerating or outright lying. She'll talk about the most intimate things. Dealers will come up to you and say things like, "So, you got a mole on your . . ." You get the idea.

But the worst part of it is the dirty looks you get from her and her friends. Hey, some people don't belong together. We make mistakes. I never hit Barbara, never even raised my voice. There were things about her that annoyed me, just like there were things about me that annoyed her. It was fun at first, but then when we got together we talked about work and the people at work and the players. It was just like being at work, one big bitch session. Maybe I'm a romantic, but I think a relationship should be some kind of sanctuary, a refuge away from the asylum. I wonder what Barbara's friends would think if they heard the juicy gossip she told me about them. Who'd be son-of-a-bitching who then?

I learned my lesson.

UNDATED

When I first broke into the business, one of the bosses said to me, "You won't find love on the other side of a layout." I kept that advice close, maybe too close. I looked for love, as the song goes, "in all the wrong places." I dated bosses, dealers, more bosses, more dealers. I married twice, thought I was in love four times, was in love twice, never put the whole package together. One day I was forty-five, with two kids in college, and still pumping cards.

Each of my husbands cheated on me. I cheated on one of them. The temptation was always there. It's the old thing about if your sex life's no good, there's someone looking to make it better. And aren't we supposed to have great sex lives? Go to the movies and find out. I don't know what those men are doing to women up on the big screens, but no one ever made me feel like a movie star.

I contracted gonorrhea once. The jerk didn't even tell me about it. I had to get a severe infection before I knew. I wasn't so much mad at him for giving it to me—after all, it takes two and all that—as I was that he just didn't tell me so that I could go to the doctor. He was a boss. I had to see him three days a week after that for the next two years. He even hit on me again. I asked him if he had another dose of the clap he wanted to pass on. Men in this business, they've got one hand up your dress and the other on their zipper and one eye on the next pretty face. They're all so horny, you'd think a few of them would know how the hell to do it.

The bosses can pressure you in subtle ways. You know, show you a little extra attention, come around and visit when business is slow, or make your job easier or harder, too. The thing with men bosses is that they seem to need some woman, an attractive or sexy one, to validate who they are. Being a shift boss or a casino manager isn't enough. Don't let anyone lie to you, the big bosses get first choice when a pretty woman gets hired. I've seen it time and time again, although there are no statistics out there to back me up.

I went with a casino manager once. He was married. I wasn't. I don't know what I was looking for. I got early outs and whatever schedule I wanted, and, of course, the pitboss and shift boss treated me gentle as a mink-lined bomb. But casino managers come and go. This one left. Fired. He found a job a week later working the floor at the Sahara for about a third of his old salary. He wanted to keep up the affair, him working another shift and playing house with his wife. After him, I quit seeing bosses. It seemed wiser. I had more friends and less stress.

The best thing about being my age is that I don't get that kind of attention anymore. Too many young ones out there. The worst thing about being my age is that I don't get that kind of attention anymore. Hey, I'm just being honest. I wouldn't go back mostly because I can't. But if I did, I'd look for love on the *other* side of the layout, either that or find another occupation.

1986

I ran around with Patty and Sandy. We were inseparable. We worked the same shift together dealing blackjack for seven years. We still talk on the phone at least once a week and get together when we can.

Sandy was wild, but Patty was as cold as a frozen slab of meat. I'm not criticizing her. In fact, we admired that about her. If she wanted something, she'd do whatever it took to get her way. We laughed at the things we did. Sandy changed boyfriends to suit a new wardrobe. Her father was an old-timer in the business and had a lot of juice, so Sandy didn't need a friend high up. She liked wild men like drug dealers and bikers and barroom brawlers. She loved to see men fight and told us stories that made our hair stand on end, like the one where she and her boyfriend were at a bar, and some guy looked at her. She went to the bathroom and on the way told the guy she wanted to see him by the telephones. He followed her. When she went back to sit by her boyfriend, she told him the other guy had followed her to the ladies' room and waited outside for her. She said men were insane lovers after they had a good fight. Like I said, she was the crazy one.

Patty played men in a different way. She used sex. One day we all went out to lunch. She was distracted, kept bitching about her needing a week off and not being able to schedule it. We left Cafe Michelle in her car. She drove straight to the casino. We asked her what we were doing there. She told us to go to the lounge and have a drink, she'd explain in a few minutes. We waited, and when she came back she said we could go now. She was much happier.

In the car we asked her what all that had been about. She smiled and said she got her vacation, that she'd gone right to the general manager himself. All it took was five minutes. Oral sex, she explained. No one would believe the story, except since everything came out about President Clinton, anyone with any brains knows the world works that way. At least it did for Patty.

I'm not going to tell any stories about myself. I will say that from time to time I had an experience that made Patty and Sandy laugh. I've been in the business thirty years now. It's changed, and it hasn't. It's hard to keep friendships, but the three of us are still friends. Part of the reason is the wildness we've shared. The business can be pretty dull, the same thing all the time. You have to stir up your own excitement, or have crazy friends.

1982

This one guy at the Showboat fell in love with a woman dealer. She was all right on the eyes and all, but not the beauty he thought she was. Anyhow, he was gone on her. They went out for about two months. In that two months he bought her $38,000 worth of jewelry. That wiped him out, all of his savings. We didn't make that much at the 'Boat, so he must have scrimped for years to save it. As soon as the money was gone, she dumped him. It was hard to feel sorry for him.

UNDATED

How are men and women in this business different? I'll tell you. I've known this particular woman as a friend for years. She's smart, the smartest person I ever worked with in a casino. She's a boss now. One night she was talking about another woman boss where she works now. She said the woman's name, but I wasn't listening very closely. She talked about how competent the woman was and how she was now the craps boss on her shift and all of the men respected her. She mentioned that this same woman had worked where I used to work. I put two and two together and came up with an entirely different picture of the same woman.

Yes, June had worked with me before.

I told my friend the story of how June, my floor boss at the time, had closed a game down to send someone to help the dealer on a busy roulette game at 6:15 one evening. We were working four dealers for three games at the time, but that turned us into a three-person crew. I was scheduled for the 6:40 break and the early out. At 6:20 Darlene came back in the pit. She was supposed to take out the dealer who'd gone to roulette. In the event of his absence, I was supposed to be tapped out to go on break, which meant I wouldn't get the early out, that the next dealer in line would get it. We prized our early outs, but I accepted what had happened.

Now, June and Darlene were best friends. They stepped away from the center of the pit and whispered. The next thing I knew Darlene was leaving the pit on a double break. Well, that was fine with me, too. It meant I'd get the early out after all. So I waited out the twenty minutes, pumping cards to one player. When the twenty minutes was up, the dealers poured out of the back room, smashed out their cigarettes, and headed for the various pits, all except Darlene.

Instead of the early out, instead of any kind of break, I stayed on the game dealing for an hour and twenty minutes and left work with sore feet and a sore back. I finished explaining this to my friend. She shook her head and said, "Get used to it. It's our turn now." When I argued that what June had done was unethical, my friend said it didn't matter, that she'd do the same thing for a woman friend. And claimed that it was the same kind of crap that men had been doing for years. I told her that I'd spent an hour and twenty minutes on a game many times besides that one, but those had been human error, and I usually got an apology or an extra break. This was intentionally done to grant one person privilege at the expense of another.

"Just get used to it," my friend said. "Who said the world was fair?"

1980?

There was a time when you could order anything you wanted without stepping outside of the casino. It was insane, literally insane. Yet everyone pretended like it wasn't happening. The bosses looked the other way. So did security. As long as dealers didn't nod off on the game, drugs were tolerated. I broke in at the Flamingo Capri, which is now the Imperial Palace. This was in the early seventies. We had three blackjack games and one craps table. I was so green. I got the job right out of dealers' school, minimum wage plus tips.

I thought, here I am, working on the Las Vegas Strip. We made seven dollars in tips my first night. One of the dealers, a craps dealer, had been watching me off and on. I was single and female, and, well, it was the seventies. There was a place called Dirty Sally's on the corner of Spring Mountain and the Strip. He asked if I wanted to go there for a drink. What else could you do with seven bucks? I said sure. We first went to the Holiday, which was also pretty new and small then, because he had free drink coupons. He seemed like a nice guy. He was a couple of years older than me and cute. He had great hair, movie-star hair, medium brown and slightly over the collar, and these great-looking hands. He made me laugh with a few of his stories about the casino. We get our free drinks and walk back to the Flamingo Capri and walk to the parking lot. We still have our drinks in hand.

We get to the parking lot, and he hands me two pills and says I should take them. I ask what they are. He calls them quacks or ducks or something and asks me where I'm from. I say Indiana. He nods. I take one of the pills and hand him the other. I asked him if he was going to take one, but he smiled at me and said he was already high. I remember going to Dirty Sally's in his car. I remember dancing one dance with him. But after that everything is a blur. I woke up in his bed.

I suppose today it's fair to call the cops and say I was raped. I mean, I was, and now it's called drug rape. But in those days no one thought of calling the cops. Fortunately, he lived a short distance from the Flamingo Capri. I dressed and got my car, then went home and showered. Three, four times, I can't remember. I couldn't shower enough times.

I went to work. He was there. I couldn't look at him, but I noticed that every time I looked up he was looking in my direction. I got scared, but what could I say? I quit the job at the end of the shift. It took me two weeks to find another dealing job at the Four Queens downtown. I found out I was pregnant about a month and a half after that encounter. I went back to him and said I was pregnant. He said, "Sure you are."

I got an abortion. Four years later I'm working at the Frontier, and who do they hire in craps? The guy who drugged me and got me pregnant. He was still kind of cute, but not the way he had been before. He looked beat or bored like he was ready to yawn any second. Within a week he hit on me. He didn't even recognize me. My hair was longer and frosted, and I'd put on fifteen pounds. I told him I'd be happy to meet him someplace after work. So we agreed to meet at Eppie's across from the university. I really wanted to confront him, but in the end I stood him up and went home.

The next shift, he was giving me the evil eye, but he still didn't remember. He got off work an hour before I did, but he waited around. When I saw him waiting in employee parking, I turned around and got a security guard to walk me to my car. I decided I had to confront him and the longer I put it off, the worse it was going to be.

It was about a week later that I saw him alone in the dining hall. I got some coffee and walked over to his table. He sneered at me as he looked up. I figured there was no point in sitting, that I could say what I had to say standing up.

"You don't remember me," I said. I went on to tell him that I was the girl he'd drug raped and gotten pregnant when he worked at the Flamingo Capri.

He said he didn't remember, and he honestly didn't. Imagine that. He didn't remember, and I couldn't forget. This time I didn't have to quit my job. He got fired. Apparently he'd lost several jobs the same way. He'd get drugged up and just forget to come to work.

3

GEORGES, STIFFS, FREAKS

If you were to ask a dealer what kept her dealing, the response most likely would be the Georges. Georges—"G" for "generous"—the big tippers. If you were to ask the same dealer what was the worst part of the job, she'd say the stiffs or describe some aberrant behavior or other demonstrated by a player, especially the high roller, whose worst behavior is notoriously tolerated. From the rich to the famous, such as Frank Sinatra, players are noted for their monumental generosity, stinginess, self-centeredness, and downright meanness.

Frank Sinatra once cost a dealer and a boss their jobs in Atlantic City because he insisted on having his cards dealt to him from a hand instead of a shoe, which is a violation of New Jersey's gaming regulations. Sinatra was notorious for bullying the little guy. In Las Vegas he was either loved or despised, with good reason either way. He brought in the high rollers and sometimes humiliated the working guy or gal. At the Sands, which he helped make famous, the story about his escapade on the golf cart was well circulated, as was the story about Carl Cohen punching him in the mouth and loosening his caps. To many who'd been humiliated by Sinatra's self-indulgent behavior, Carl Cohen, even twenty years later, was considered a champion of the little guy.

Image is everything in Las Vegas. Part of that image is that casinos protect their customers from outside scrutiny. Casinos don't want to receive adverse publicity or to be associated with any story that lends itself to controversy. Taking pictures in casinos has traditionally been banned as one way to protect players from outside intrusions. The stakes are too high to risk offending a big player. The competition for them is fierce. At many casinos high rollers can negotiate terms, like ninety days' or six months' credit, babysitters for the children, three suites, a private maid, and, not so long ago, a prostitute or two. So valuable are they that they are courted like royalty and protected like children. Many stories of high rollers have been lost; others are suppressed. Some of the stories include drug use and sexual deviation—not the stuff the marketing department wants spread on newspaper headlines.

Of course, what constitutes a high roller varies from casino to casino. A top player at Harrah's, Las Vegas, might not qualify for a free breakfast at Caesars Palace. Some casinos don't want to risk the high-end losses associated with some players. They would consider taking them on as customers, but only on the condition that they lose—a term that no high roller will accede to. The rich players are as quirky and as normal as any other casino customer; it's a matter of style and budget. One is sacrificing a fishing trip to Ensenada, the other delaying an expedition to Mount Everest or building a third estate home in Hawaii.

If high rollers are at the top of the food chain, dealers are at the bottom. Yet there exists a strange saprophytic relationship between the dominant feeder and the quick prey. Even in a theoretically classless society, someone has to cater to the whims of the wealthy. How else can their status be confirmed? Dealers are at the mercy of the high rollers, but a good dealer works this to his advantage by giving the player what he or she most desires—recognition, the VIP treatment. "Hello, Mr. D. How are you? I heard you were in the hotel. Did you bring the wife?" These words spark life into the eyes of the high roller. This is Las Vegas. Here he's king, she's queen.

Nowhere in a casino is obsequious behavior more on stage than in a baccarat pit, where dealers wear all the trappings of the trade: three-hundred-dollar tuxedos, patent leather shoes, and syrupy smiles. Some baccarat dealers make upward of a hundred thousand a year, and in a good year even more. Pretense abounds. It's a game inside a game, and everyone's playing. Hustle, posture, hustle. Gone are the days when dealers popped crisp hundred-dollar bills down next to a line of greenbacks. Now they use chips, but the show goes on, and crowds still gather about the railings to watch and fantasize as the haute of pop culture perform. It is another world just as surely as Disneyland is another world.

The noisiest spot in any casino is where the dice are rolling. The craps player is a different breed from the blackjack or baccarat player, so the hustle's different, harder. The rewards are high here, too, if a crew can hold it together. In some casinos dealers have to make layoffs to the person sitting box or the floor person to look the other way while the crew hustles the player. There's a game inside the game here as well. Craps is demanding and the payoffs complicated, so the dealer has a notable advantage over the player. Some high rollers simply buy in and tell the dealers to place the bets for them. And the dealers do, not neglecting to place a bet for themselves along the way. It's all perfectly acceptable. This is not to suggest that life in the craps pit is a mini-heaven. At the Sands, years ago, a high roller used to come in five to ten times a year for three to five days at a stay. He'd reserve a table to himself, sit on a stool, and win or lose, roll hand after hand after hand. In twenty-five years he never tipped a crew. The ones who had to deal to him looked bleached out when they left at the end of the shift. One dealer said that player couldn't be hustled with a Bowie knife and a .38.

For sheer meanness, though, the reward goes to blackjack players who are so inclined. The blackjack player can literally hold a dealer captive for hours. Here the interplay is more personal, and often the dealer is held in some way responsible for the outcome. Confrontations are more frequent in the blackjack pit, tips are shared, the work more monotonous, and the income lower. Often players expect to be entertained. Cards change faster than weather on the Plains. The pace of the game and cramped seating create a kind of intimacy. Here the axiom that "intimacy creates contempt" applies. When the stakes go up, the situation is compounded. Any dealer will tell you that the nicest players still hate to lose. They sometimes take it personally. But there are players who come by nastiness quite naturally. No arena better affords them the opportunity to act out than a blackjack game.

Dealers are reminded many times over the period of a month that they are on the bottom of the food chain, where they have to feel fortunate to gather up the crumbs that fall off the table. On the other hand, where else can a person without a high school diploma earn forty to a hundred thousand a year by turning over cards and remembering a high roller's name? The casino is a world of opposites in operation—hope and despair, generosity and stinginess, kindness and cruelty.

1988

It was hot already, a summer like most in Vegas, maybe hotter. Bob said the pigeons were packing for Canada; that's how hot it was. Every July is hot, and every July money got bad in the casino. This year was the worst yet, maybe for temperature, too. We were making thirty a day in wages and maybe forty in tips, and the casino was so dead most of the time we could have bowled in the aisles. Those of us who had savings, who prepared ourselves for the bad months of July and August, were already deep into our reserves. Others, the ones who spent it as they got it, were buried. Some were borrowing from shylocks to make the mortgage or pay the power bill, and power bills are important to pay when it's 115 degrees.

All the talk in the dealers' room was about money or, more precisely, the lack of it. What happened? This was the Sands, wasn't it, home of the Rat Pack and the Copa Girls? Now tour buses pulled into the south lot and opened their doors. Out poured streams of blue-haired ladies from San Diego and Vietnamese from Costa Mesa. They hit the tables with three-for-two coupons and asked for discount tickets to the buffet or cranked quarters into the slots. The bells rang, the dollars and quarters rattled in the slot trays, then two hours later, fed and grumbling, the bus gamblers were herded onto the buses and the casino was once again empty. We'd stand at our dead games, cards fanned out like a Chinese painting, and stare off as the band in the lounge played "Tie a Yellow Ribbon," as if it were the only song they knew.

We were getting scared. Layoffs were rumored, and no one hires in Vegas during the summer, especially bad summers. The big question was how much was an unemployment check based on thirty dollars a day. Three dealers quit to take jobs in Atlantic City, a true act of desperation. We were getting lazy, too, and angry. When a stiff landed on our games, we fired cards at his hands as if we were trying to drive nails, aimed for his knuckles and let fly. Or to release our irritation, we banged chips against the edge of the rack as we went out to pay off a winner. Where were the Georges? We talked about the golden days of the Sands and lamented their passing. The high rollers had gone to Caesars or the Hilton or the MGM, a few to the Tropicana and Desert Inn.

One morning in the middle of that hot July he walked in and landed on Caroline's blackjack game. Oh, sure, she told us later, he was a case, looked like someone swept up off the stadium floor after a Grateful Dead concert, long ponytail, blue jeans, torn T-shirt. He carried a shopping bag. She was tempted to tell him that no brown bagging was allowed. She said hello and shuffled her cards. He opened his bag, turned it upside down, and dumped the contents out. Bills scattered over the layout—one-hundred-dollar bills.

Caroline's tongue could turn small talk into money the same way Jascha Heifetz's fingers could turn catgut into music. She saw those hundreds, and the gab started flowing. By the time she had the twenty-three thousand counted down and stuffed in the drop box, she was telling him about her third grade teacher, and he seemed interested. The rest of us craned our necks to watch the action. Caroline told the guy he needed some coffee and suggested he take a seat. He took the coffee but didn't sit down.

He was as lame a player as any who'd ever walked into a Strip casino. He hit a fourteen against a five, didn't know about doubling down, thought he needed a jack and an ace or it wasn't really a blackjack. When she paid him time and a half for a queen-ace snapper, he tried to give half the money back, two hundred and fifty dollars, to be exact. Caroline glanced over her shoulder at Jimmy, a boss, who was a nice enough guy, but when money hit the layout, he turned into the biggest sweater in the joint. Bob said Jimmy was such a sweater that his DNA was two-thirds angora wool, one-third cotton yarn. Caroline noticed beads of sweat forming on Jimmy's brow and knew it wasn't a good time to hustle a toke. But this was the summer of our worst drought. She smiled at "the bagman" and said, "It's yours unless you want to give it to me."

He looked at the chips, at her, sat down, read her name tag and said, "What the hell." He handed her the two-fifty.

When she came off the game for her first break, Jimmy grabbed her and demanded to know what the hell that was all about.

"About me feeding my kids, Jimmy. If you had kids and needed money, you'd understand."

Jimmy had to bend. Times were that tough. The best joint on the

Strip was now a bus stop, and he knew what we were going through. To take himself off the hook, he grumbled something about the eye in the sky wanting to know if Caroline was hustling.

"Tell him yeah, and I'm proud of it," she said.

It could have cost her the job, but no dealer in the place would have ever talked to Jimmy again. Besides, he'd been there in the good days when the dealers laid off a few tokes on the bosses. Two or three Ben Franklins in an envelope had compromised the virtue of more than one sweater. Jimmy had gotten his share, had drunk and gambled a lot of it away, but he'd looked the other way when it was to his benefit. We knew it, so did he.

In the break room Caroline was all smiles. She was glib and knew how to tell a story, but this story was telling itself. The bottom line was that she had dropped almost a thousand in the toke box, and the bagman had piles in front of him. Someone turned on the TV, and we argued over whether to watch a soap opera or baseball. Things were getting back to normal.

The bagman played for another hour or so. He asked Jimmy for the time. Jimmy said it was almost one o'clock. The bagman said he didn't know what to do with the chips, so Caroline pointed to the cage. He nodded, said he was in a big hurry, and pushed them toward Caroline. He asked if she could cash them for him.

"No," she said.

He nodded, looked at the front door, and grimaced.

"You keep them," he said.

There was almost nine thousand in chips in front of him. She asked if he was sure. He said he'd had a good time and enjoyed her company and would be back.

We popped a three-hundred-plus envelope the next day, not nearly enough to get caught up, but more than enough to restore our faith in mankind—at least for a day or two. Caroline was a hero. She told the story over and over, but no one told her to stop. It was a good story.

Two days later the Bagman, as we now called him, returned with a fresh bag full of fresh Ben Franklins. This went on for several weeks, not every day but every three or so. He was the golden goose. We could pay some bills now. We weren't getting rich, but breathing easier and arguing over sports or gossiping about the latest facelift on one of the cocktail waitresses. The mystery now was who the Bagman was. He refused to give a name. This was the year that the IRS pressed a policy on casinos that they had to report any player who bought in for more than ten thousand dollars over a twenty-four-hour span. After that first day the Bagman never brought more than nine thousand, nine hundred dollars to the table. Someone had wised him up.

It was the same most every time he came. Still dressed in blue jeans and T-shirt, brown bag in hand, he'd wander in and find Caroline. If she wasn't working, he'd trip from table to table looking for someone to pass the time with. There was no need to hustle him by then; first bet out of the chute, he had the dealers up for at least fifty dollars. He never talked about himself, but he wanted to hear a little bit about the dealer who was turning over the cards, said he wanted to know the kind of person who was taking his money. The money seemed to mean nothing to him.

The bosses were constantly on Caroline to find out what the Bagman's real name was. They had her in the office several times, quizzing her as if she were holding back information. But the truth is she didn't know. Then he stopped coming in. And a week later we all found out who he was. His trial for drug smuggling took place that week in federal court. He was convicted and held over for sentencing.

Of course, we had all suspected as much. Dirty money, some would say. Probably. He fed some kids, helped pay some mortgages, gave us something to speculate about when we were talking in the break room. The federal judge sent the Bagman away for more than two decades. He was about forty when he was sentenced, had made a fortune. Maybe some of it is waiting for him at the end of his sentence. Who knows? I don't know if he had money left or a conscience either, but he had a heart. The casino's gone, the Bagman's still doing time, Caroline's cutting hair, but that summer happened just the way things always seem to happen, out of the blue. Ask any old-timers who once worked at the Sands. They'd remember the Bagman.

1970s

Jimmy Chagra used to play here [Caesars Palace] in the seventies. You never saw anything like him then, except here. Cash player. Two, three, four thousand a hand. He'd lay the money down on the square and say, "Deal," and we'd ask, "To the limit?," meaning his limit, whatever it was that night. And he was a pretty nice guy, a partier, and a hell of a George. As soon as he got a step on the house, he spread it around like we were his family. It was nothing for us to find five or six hundred in the envelope when Jimmy was playing. Not everyone could deal to him. He had his favorites. I only dealt to him on occasion.

One night I'm dealing to him, and he goes belly up. Not even a roller-coaster ride. A straight plunge downward from the first bet. About a quarter of a million gone in an hour. He's got the table reserved and a room for two days. He asks for a pit phone, which the pit boss brings. That extension cord stretched over me, resting on my shoulder like I was some kind of utility pole. And I stand there staring off like I *am* one. He gives the operator a number in Texas to call—he was from El Paso—and he tells the guy on the other end he needs three hundred thousand cash on a plane and brought to him right away. The guy on the other end says something to Jimmy, and Jimmy laughs. He tells the guy to say hi to the dealer and hands me the phone. The guy on the other end says that I should take it easy on Jimmy because he's on an allowance, no more than a hundred thousand a day. I say "no problem," and we all laugh. What did I care if I had to wait? I got to stay on the game and do nothing but listen to Jimmy talk it up with the bosses and the cocktail waitresses. He was a good-looking guy, too, and the ladies took to him.

That money was there in three hours. If I'm lying, I'm dying. Jimmy had a private jet and a pilot who got up out of bed and flew a runner here. The runner walks down the aisle with two briefcases and brings them to the game. Jimmy opens one case. Doesn't count anything, just takes the first three stacks, lays them on the squares, and says, "Time to earn your bread, man." I holler out that money plays to the limit and shuffle.

We knew he was using drug money. Where else would you get that kind of money in the seventies? Besides, look at who was running the joints in those days, and that was before the Asians started coming over and making five thousand dollars on a hand seem like petty change (but they don't treat us like we're relatives, I'll tell you). Who knows, maybe some of them got their money from drugs, too. I always wonder about anyone with a lot of cash. So does the IRS these days. It's just not the same.

Anyhow, Jimmy did finally buy himself a house here in Vegas. I can't remember where exactly, but after he was arrested for drugs and that judge in Texas got hit, everyone at work speculated about that house.

Jimmy hid his money somewhere. Who knows? It could be there, a fortune or two. Or maybe nothing. I heard his brother got killed, too, a hit or in a robbery or something. He was an attorney back in Texas. Maybe he was the guy who said Jimmy was on an allowance. I don't know. You don't ask questions. The job was worth sixty grand a year. You keep your mouth shut and deal, smile when they tip you and remember who's George and who's not.

Funny, Jimmy's doing life, and so's Woody Harrelson's dad, Charles Harrelson. He was the trigger man who did the judge. They're doing a life stretch each, and I'm still doing my time behind the game, thirty-four years now. You see, I was a player, too. Not cards or craps. Stocks. What didn't get wiped out during Carter got wiped out with Reagan and Bush. Funny, people hate Clinton, but I damn sure wish I'd had the money in the market now that I had in it in the '70s and '80s. Wonder how much Jimmy's got buried. Wonder if he'll ever see it. Oh, well, he had the sweet life for a while. How many of us can say that?

1987

I never knew her name. We just called her the Dragon Lady. She had a temperament that was half fire and half poison. Every dealer in the joint hated her. One even told the bosses they could fire him if they wanted to, but he wasn't going to deal another hand to her. He didn't get fired, but it created a problem because other dealers started balking about going in on the game if she was playing. Once a boss sent a Vietnamese woman dealer to the Dragon Lady's table. The temperamental player snatched some cards from the discard rack, tore them up, and threw them in the air. She wouldn't let women deal to her or Asians, male or female, so the Asians and the females were all excused, and the only ones left were white and black males. The women dealers showed no sympathy toward us males. One said it was what men had coming for being the pigs they were.

I had no desire to go on the game the day of my blowup with the Dragon Lady, but I did. The casino books the bets and pays the winners, and that's what makes the paycheck come home. I'd dealt to her before, and, yes, it was every kind of pain short of physical torture a human can endure, but a shift is only eight hours, and I had survived my past encounters. At least that was my thinking.

She was already stuck, not in the grave exactly, but down forty or fifty grand. I buried a card and waited for her to bet. But she just sat there sipping a straw in a glass of ice and stared at me about as hatefully as one human can at another. I remembered seeing as a kid old reruns of *Flash Gordon*. She reminded me of the evil Ming. I figured I was there for eight hours, and if it took her that long to bet, all the better. No sweat off me. Finally she spoke.

"You think you one hot motherfucker," she said. "You not. You not shit. You not even a piece of dirt under my fingernail."

I didn't say anything.

She stood. "You think you better than me?" She held out her hand for me to see the rings on her fingers. One diamond was about three carats.

I looked at the diamond and asked, "How many batteries does that take?"

She cranked her arm back and heaved the glass she'd been sipping out of. It missed me, cleared the pit, and hit a slot machine somewhere. By then she had gone completely berserk, throwing around profanity and threats. The pitboss came over and tried to calm her. He kept asking her to relax, but she didn't slow down a bit. The shift boss and two security guards arrived, but she held them at bay with her threats. Players at nearby games gathered up their chips and moved farther away. It took most of ten minutes to get her calm enough to ask her what had provoked the incident. What the bosses really wanted to know was what I had said, but she really didn't know. She kept pointing to her rings and muttering that I'd insulted her. Her explanations weren't lucid, and the more she tried to explain what I'd said the worse her accent got. Finally the shift boss asked me what had happened. I told him about the batteries. He cupped his hand over his eyes and shook his head. The way he acted, shaking his head and clicking his tongue in his cheek, you'd think I'd threatened her or called her a name, maybe vowed to kill all her posterity or something. He told me to see him when I went on break.

She sat down and started playing as if nothing had happened. And I did my best to deal as if nothing had happened, all the while thinking how sick this all was.

I found the shift boss on my break, but when I asked what he wanted, he merely dismissed me with a wave of the hand. After the break, I went back to the same game. The Dragon Lady was waiting for me. She said that I would be lucky for her, and if I wasn't, she would have me fired.

I dealt the cards. If she lost a hand, she tore those cards in two. If she won a hand, she threw the cards at me. No one intervened. No one told her that her behavior was inappropriate. No one cared about anything but the chips that went her way or came back to the house. She won most of what she had lost. When my hour was up, my feet were burning, and my back was sore. I was particularly grateful to see my relief enter the pit. He tapped me out, and I started to clap. As I raised my hand, the Dragon Lady dropped a five-dollar check in front of me and asked for change. I gave her five dollars.

"Here, for you," she said, setting a dollar token on the layout. "You lucky me."

I took the token to the dealers' box and dropped it. A woman dealer saw what I'd dropped and asked if that was all I got for all the money I'd given out.

"No," I said, "I got that for taking all the bullshit you don't have to."

She said that now I knew the kind of crap women had to take every day.

Some time later that same week the casino barred the Dragon Lady from playing and asked her to leave. By that time she'd been banned from playing in so many other casinos that there remained only a handful where she was still welcome. I heard that she started playing at the Imperial Palace, and then a few weeks, perhaps two months, later a rumor circulated that she'd been found dead, the victim of a robbery or foul play. It's hard to put teeth into rumors, but I remember hoping it was true. Sick as it sounds, it seemed fitting at the time.

1979?

I was on this twenty-five-dollar-minimum game dealing to a cocktail waitress from Caesars. She was a beauty. It was a graveyard shift about five in the morning. You could see she'd been out hitting the rounds for the night and had been drinking a bit, but she was okay. She was betting somewhere between twenty-five and a hundred. This guy, some Midwesterner probably, really square, was watching her play. It was easy to see he wasn't interested in the way she was playing or if she was winning.

He watched her for about twenty minutes. Later I figured out that he was just trying to build up his courage. His hand went for the billfold, and he counted out a twenty and a five-dollar bill, which he placed on the betting square nearest her bet. He sat down. I called out money plays. He looked over at her.

"That's really beautiful perfume you're wearing, Miss," he said. "Is it Oriental?"

She didn't break stride. She leaned close to him and said, "Yeah. I just got through giving head to some Oriental."

The guy didn't know what the hell to say. He played the hand out about half dazed and looked happy that he lost so he could leave.

1986

I'll call him "Mr. K." He was a television executive, a large man with money to burn and big appetites—gambling being one, the others being drugs and alcohol. But gambling wasn't satisfying in itself. What was the point, what was at stake if he could lose hundreds of thousands and the loss was meaningless? So when he came to play, he made it a challenge, a show of sorts, him against the house. He made his own rules, improvising as he played, and whatever he contrived, no matter how outlandish, the bosses went along with it. It actually got pretty amusing.

When Mr. K arrived, the shift boss turned most of his other duties over to a pitboss and followed Mr. K around. It was a sight, the boss following him around as if led by a leash. We knew when Mr. K was coming because the evening before he arrived, a young Israeli, a former wheel dealer, would show up and start playing roulette. He was Mr. K's cocaine pusher. He could get by with almost anything and did because Mr. K's impunity transferred to him as well. He'd load up the table with his friends, buy all six colors—two hundred each—and they'd start stacking chips on the layout. None of them would bet until the ball was spun, and when the ball dropped, they'd still be plunking stacks of chips on the layout. If one of their numbers didn't hit, they'd scream that the dealer didn't give them enough time to bet. On more than one occasion, the bosses allowed them to place bets after the number was called, place the chips on the winning number, any amount they wanted up to two hundred dollars.

Later, after the cocaine dealer proved that the bosses could be in-timidated, Mr. K got wind of the action and jumped into the foray. Dealing the wheel got crazy, signing markers, pushing out stack after stack on payoffs, raking in a thousand chips a spin, paying winners up to the maximum on propositions, and sometimes watching late bets go down and being helpless to do anything because the bosses were right there watching and nodding for you to go ahead and pay. The payoffs challenged the most nimble-minded dealers—ninety-four on the streets, one hundred seven on the corners, forty-seven on the splits, eighty-three straight up—and they wanted the payoffs totaled and converted. If the dealer made a mistake, Mr. K's friends demanded an apology. The bosses never raised an eyebrow. It was surreal.

Early on Mr. K didn't tip and never talked to the dealers, but after he discovered that the bosses didn't want high rollers going overboard when toking the dealers, he took tipping on as a personal campaign. This, too, became part of the game. I guess he viewed us as protago-nists in his war against the casino. He was unpredictable. Occasionally he'd blow up over nothing and start shouting; other times he'd lose a hundred thousand and walk away smiling. The dealers never knew if he was going to stiff them or hand over a thousand dollars in chips or put them up for a twenty-five-dollar bet. His cocaine dealer would get crazy whenever Mr. K tipped a dealer. The dealers got almost as much satisfaction over that as they did over being toked.

One night Mr. K and his cocaine dealer had been drinking and snort-ing cocaine all day and much of the shift. They were gambling, just the two of them, on roulette. Mr. K went to the bathroom, and when he returned a film of white powder was smeared on his nostrils and the tip of his nose. The dealer leaned over the table and pointed this out to him. Mr. K was wearing a short-sleeved knit shirt. He grabbed the co-caine dealer's sleeve and wiped his nose on it. The shift boss shook his head.

Another night Mr. K was so drunk that he urinated into a planter by the baccarat table. Security had to escort him up to his room. Some-where along the way, Mr. K and the casino parted company, whether by mutual agreement or not, no one ever said, but he went elsewhere and took his cocaine dealer with him. The dealers had mixed feelings about his leaving. Some had come to actually like him, but mostly it was the occasional score that came their way when he was gambling that they missed. Sometime later one of the dealers came upon Mr. K's cocaine dealer at a club called The Hop and waited for him in the parking lot. That's another story. As for Mr. K, the last I'd heard he'd come down with terminal cancer and was doing his best to keep the party going to the end. Maybe that's what it's all about.

1987?

We had this busty woman with no bra on the craps game at the Aladdin. It was busy, the dice were rolling for the players, and she had them. She was wearing a halter top, screaming and bouncing around like she'd just been granted a divorce and a million-dollar settlement. I sent her the dice. She shook them and jumped up and down. Just as she got ready to throw, her halter straps came loose, both of them. But she was bent over and looking up at the other end of the table. There she was, breasts hanging out and so excited about rolling the dice she didn't realize it. Everyone else did, though. All the action stopped except hers. The dice went down the table. It was my job to watch them, but I didn't. And neither did the box man. We were all staring at her. She was still jumping up and down, her breasts putting on a hell of a show, when she noticed. She pulled up her top, held it firmly, and asked what the number was. No one knew.

1974

This was the Stardust when the Mob ran the place. On a craps game. I know it happened even if I didn't see it because three of my buddies told me the same story, and one of them was on the game. My friend was on the base dealing at the time this happened to a stick man.

The dice were rolling for the house—point, seven, point, seven. It was brutal on the players; no one left. There was one player who was in seven or eight hundred and hadn't won a bet. The guy on the mop called a seven, and the other two dealers, my pal being one of them, swept up the checks. The dice went out, and a player made a point, a six or an eight, an easy point. The dealers were talking up place bets. As they were laying the bets and the stick man was calling for props, this guy opened his jacket and pulled out a gun—a revolver. He looked at the guy on the stick and told him not to call another seven. The whole game went stone dead, just like someone had announced that the Russians had launched missiles at us. No one could believe it. The guy with the gun told the stick man to get the dice rolling and not to dare call a seven. The stick man shakes his head. The guy with the gun said, "I told you to move them." But the stick man wasn't going to move the dice if God told him to. He'd take his chances that way rather than call another seven. It was a stand-off for several minutes.

Someone in the pit had the good sense to call security. They surrounded the guy with the gun before he could react and lifted him up, then managed to disarm him and drag him away. In the meantime, the guy on the stick figured he'd literally dodged a bullet, and, in a sense, that was what he'd done. A half-hour went by, and the guy with the gun showed up with a casino executive who said that everything was worked out, that it was okay for the guy to play, that security had his gun. Turns out the guy was Mob, from Chicago. The whole affair was hushed up. Just like something on television, but with irony.

UNDATED

I had this Cuban come to my game with a briefcase full of hundreds. I knew he was Cuban because I'm Mexican and can recognize accents. He opened the briefcase and started betting, "money plays" on three and four hands. I'd been dealing a long while, and this was the Sands where we were used to big play, but this Cuban topped everything. He bet and bet and bet. How much, I can't be sure, but I'll bet it was over a quarter of a million. He won a handful of bets was all, was on a terrible losing streak when he had three twenties on three hands, and I had an ace showing. I think he had two thousand bet on each hand. He took insurance on all three hands. I had an ace in the hole as well. I picked up the insurance bets, three thousand, and locked that up, then turned over my hand and hit it with two more aces and a seven. The Cuban went berserk.

He didn't have the good sense to leave with anything. It was pride. Macho. He took it personally. It was me he wanted to beat, but you can't beat the cards. How much did he lose? More than would fit into the drop box. I couldn't put any more money into it. Security had to cart it away and give me credit slips, and I couldn't even get those to drop. That's the worst hit I ever saw a cash player take.

1980s

We called him "the Sweetheart." "The Sweetheart's here," we'd say, and everything that was grim turned bright. He'd land in the baccarat pit and put us up for a tie right off, never a second thought. He knew our names and even the names of a few of our children. He'd ask about them and wonder if we were saving for our kids' educations. He was a regular guy, only better, if you know what I mean. He lived in Los Angeles, actually Brentwood, I think. He played tennis. Once in a while, he'd show up in tennis apparel. We'd ask how his game went, and he'd just answer with a shrug. He never was one to talk about himself. Humble, you could say.

"I'm not very good at it," he once said. "My employees try to let me win, but I'm just not very good. But I bet we can beat this game."

He used "we" a lot whenever he talked about beating the game. We were on his side, and he knew it. Even the bosses were for him. Of course, they were in for the layoff whenever the Sweetheart was in. One weekend we gave over ten grand to the bosses, three of them, each night. The pitboss got four grand, while the other two picked up three apiece. I think we gave the casino shift boss two grand as well, but in the form of a Rolex. I don't know how much the cocktail waitress made, but that was the weekend the Sweetheart took the table for three million, and she couldn't bring him grapefruit juice and coffee fast enough. He caught the streak he always wanted, stayed awake almost to dawn every night, and walked out the happiest man alive.

I bet he'd be pleased to know that the money I made then is paying for my daughter's college right now, business administration, and I already put the boy through law school. How much did we make in tokes that weekend? Ten percent of what he walked away with, plus about ten thousand from other players who were in on the streak. I took home over seventy thousand, most of it on Saturday. I woke my wife up at four o'clock in the morning and dumped the money on the bedspread. Forty-two thousand we counted out. She tossed money in the air and buried her face in it. She's a country girl who didn't have milk money when she went to school. She never imagined so much money at once. Most I ever brought home before that was six thousand. We couldn't sleep. We got up out of bed and counted it again, and after we set twenty grand aside for the kids' college fund, we made a list of all the things she wanted for the house. We tiled the patio and installed a gas barbecue. No pool. I didn't want my kids drowning. I have a terrible fear of pools. When I first came to Las Vegas, I lived in the area called the Naked City. It's over by the Stratosphere. A baby boy drowned in a swimming pool. His mama left him alone for two minutes with the door open, and when she got back the baby was gone. They found him in the pool. Three years old. No pool, I said to her. Most things, I let her have her way, but not that. No pool. I took her hand and led her into the daughter's room. She was five then and sleeping like an angel. I gave my wife a hug and said to her, "The Sweetheart's done a good thing for us."

I'm a simple guy. I never expected a lot of things out of life. I got lucky. This business is a crazy one, me making all this money, and all. But I'm a family man. Take vacations with the family, even now. I've seen people make all sorts of money, and they've got nothing, some of them because of drugs. Some just because they buy everything they can, or they blow it gambling or on women or on men, depending. My wife's a good woman. I never held back a nickel of what I made. I write up one parlay ticket a week during football season. I love the Falcons, pathetic as they are. My wife approves of twenty dollars a week on football. She watches the games with me and tells me her picks, though I never bet them. She likes the Oilers, which is about as sad as liking Atlanta.

She's helped me stay close to what life's about. I think the Sweetheart would appreciate that as well. That's why when he died, I took the week off work and flew my family to the funeral. I wanted my son and daughter, and especially my wife, to pay respects to the man who made our life a lot better. It's easy for people in the business to get bitter. They forget what life is, if they ever knew. Me, I try to give everyone a chance. It's not always easy to like another person, but spending time disliking people can't be very healthy if what I've witnessed is true. I'd like to add that the Sweetheart's funeral was a fine one. Everyone spoke highly of him. I told him that the other dealers sent their best. The old-timers, me being one, talk about him even now. Guess being remembered is something. That's one good reason to have kids.

1976

Colonel Parker bet every number every way he could get to it. Sometimes so many chips were on the roulette layout that the numbers were hidden. The table was reserved for him and him alone, and the Hilton allowed him to have all the colors of the chips, each marked at a given denomination. It was virtually impossible for him to know how much he was betting on a given spin. He spread the chips until he had no more. The table was roped off. A gallery would form to watch. People were almost as intrigued with Colonel Parker as they were with Elvis.

Rumor had it that Elvis wanted to stop playing the showroom but that the Colonel was buried in markers and kept renewing the contract. They were supposed to have argued over it. The night in question the dealer had been buried for some four hours, and when he came off the break, he asked Colonel Parker if he knew he couldn't win.

"Don't have to, Son. Got me a million-dollar pair 'a sideburns making me more 'an I ever could lose to you."

The dealer went on his break, knowing it was true. Of course, the reason why Elvis never performed at other hotels is that Colonel Parker was using the contract to pay off his markers at the Hilton. The casino kept extending him credit, so the cycle went on and on. The dealer was called down from his break and told to report to the pitboss, who told him he was suspended for telling the Colonel he couldn't win.

"I asked him a question," the dealer said.

"Same thing."

The dealer, happy for the extra time off, took the two-day suspension and went fishing at Lake Mead. Years later, when the Colonel had died and Elvis had died and the dealer had been fired in a mass layoff, he told the story to another boss at a different casino.

"I heard that story," the boss told him. "But that the dealer was fired."

Knowing he was part of a Las Vegas legend, the dealer smiled.

1970s

I call the guy "Stumps." It's probably the strangest thing I ever had happen on a craps game. No. Make that in my whole life. It was at the Stardust. I was dealing on third base and busy. The dice were rolling, and I'm paying or taking every hand. This guy on my end was having a hard time reaching the table, so I helped him when I could to place a bet, etc. He tossed a quarter check down on the field, and a nine rolled. I had all sorts of bets to pay, and as I was going around I dropped his payoff in the field next to his bet. Now, dealers are not required or encouraged to hand off winners from the field, as those bets favor the house.

The guy asked me to hand him the money. I had to place the come bets and one or two call bets. I told him I'd take care of it in a second. The next thing I knew he hoisted himself up onto the table and landed next to the pass line. He had no legs, just stumps. He said, "Excuse me," and walked three steps from my left to the field and picked up his money. He said he had to go, swung himself over the side of the table and onto this platform on rollers, and took off pushing himself with his knuckles just as nonchalantly as a cat that doesn't want attention.

The box man looked up at me and asked me to take better care of my end of the table. Like that's something I had control of!

4

YOU'RE FIRED, HAVE A NICE DAY

Dealers, subject to the ever-present threat of a change in management, or whimsical shifts in personnel policies, or the arbitrary values of a given supervisor, work under a particular kind of job security-related stress, which is to say virtually no job security at all. A dealer's performance or work habits may have nothing to do with whether or not she will have a job at the start of the next shift. Each casino has its own personnel policies, its own coda or culture, and the dealers work without benefit of a union or any contract, collective or individual. Nevada has a right-to-work law and a longstanding tradition at the legislature, whose members are elected by the largesse of casinos, of defeating proworker bills. The influence of the casinos extends beyond the walls of the legislature and into the governor's office and state courts, which have not been particularly friendly to employee grievances. Additionally, longstanding efforts to unionize gaming employees have failed. At several gaming properties where a union movement got under way, dealers, because they couldn't come together in unison, undermined the elections. Elsewhere, the casinos that have gone through the process of sanctioned union votes have appealed the election results to the courts until, in virtually every case, the dealers were forced into another vote or lost or surrendered to what seemed the inevitable. The unions wear all the bruises.

I worked in the casinos off and on from 1977 to 1996. Looking back, it seems such a long stretch, but I was, from the summer of 1984, working toward leaving, so I never thought of it as a career. I had a plan, which included finishing college through a terminal graduate degree and teaching. In the meantime, I was dependent upon my income from the casinos and felt confident that I would finish my education without any financial burdens. Why should I worry? I'd never been fired, although I'd heard innumerable accounts of dealers being fired, both in individual firings and mass layoffs. I had a good work record. Being a competent dealer, who dealt four games, and a reliable employee (three sick days off in seven years and no formal customer complaints), I felt certain that I'd never be fired, at least not without cause. But at the worst possible time I was fired along with some twenty other dealers, all without cause. We were replaced by dealers who started at the low end of the pay scale without benefits for ninety days or vacations for a year. We were fired by the Maxim during the Christmas season and in a year when the casino was enjoying huge profits.

In the long run, everything worked out best for me. My plans were interrupted, but the event of my firing only fueled my determination to achieve my goals. Others were less fortunate. They had no plan, no ambition beyond the daily envelope. Although there is nothing wrong with wanting to work as a dealer, there is something naive in thinking that it is a secure vocation. Conditions are better now as far as job security goes, but this does not mean that jobs are, in any sense, secure. Firings are not as capricious as they once were. Still, all nonunion employees work without contracts and with few channels for appealing terminations. Any misinterpreted expression of individuality can still result in termination from a casino. At Harrah's, Las Vegas, a dealer who'd been an employee for twelve years was fired because he didn't smile "enough" and wasn't friendly "enough" and didn't talk "enough." He wasn't accused of rudeness or failing to deliver the mandatory greeting to customers. "Not enough" was his transgression. The campaign to fire him was initiated by an ambitious floor person who gave the three stages of warnings—one verbal, two written. The dealer lost in the appeals system because he had no witnesses to speak for him, and the arbitrary interpretation of "enough" was left up to casino management to decide.

After my firing for no cause in 1984, I distrusted the promises and assurances of anyone connected to casino management. I worked tenuously, as do all dealers, at the pleasure of corporate suits and under their rhetorical assurances of job security and fair play for all employees. I doubted every policy and every word of every supervisor. I guarded my private life and avoided controversy. Despite all my precautions, I never felt for a moment secure, and that, I believe, is how most dealers feel.

1984

In December we were fired by the Maxim, twenty or more in all, most long-time employees drawing three or four weeks' vacation a year. This was the second such purge in two years. The week we were fired, management sent down free dinner certificates to Da Vinci's, the gourmet restaurant. This was followed two days later by the first of the termination slips. Everyone was nervous. It was strange how you could look up and down the pit and sense the same thought on everyone's mind. Who's next? The bosses were noticeably absent from the casino floor. I remember turning a corner and seeing the man who ran casino surveillance. He was one of the decision makers, even though he couldn't be licensed as a key employee because of a felony conviction for theft from a casino—card cheating, at that. He looked away, and I knew my fate.

After that I just waited.

Upper management—especially Art Woods, the general manager whose background was in accounting—was continually chipping away at employees, cutting back pay scales, forcing overtime without compensation, reducing schedules, and standing dealers up to supervise games rather than hiring floor supervisors, which forced the dealers to pay for this temporary supervision out of their own tips. Equally offensive was upper management's disdain of pit supervisors. In October two years earlier, the general manager had initiated a directive that reduced the salaries of midmanagement employees by 10 percent. At year's end, everyone from shift boss up received a five-digit bonus, but the pit supervisors' salary scale wasn't reinstated. They received a turkey for Christmas. Almost a year passed before the pit supervisors' wages were reinstated. The general manager had the audacity to call it a raise. But it was better than being fired because that was just about the time the first purge was taking place.

That year, terminations became a monthly event. Dealers wondered who was going to get it next. Events took on a surreal aspect. Christmas was coming, and the dealers seemed to take one of two tracks about everything: They either went wild, buying everything they could for Christmas, many on credit, or they hoarded their money. It was the worst time of year to lose a job, but one of the easiest to find work because many casinos hire for New Year's. In late November, Art Woods issued another warning memo that read: "Layoffs and terminations will continue until morale improves." Again dealers were invited to a complimentary meal at Da Vinci's. The holiday terminations began shortly after the memo came out. None of us was let go for cause. "Change of personnel" was the reason stated on the termination slip. The shift boss called me off the game toward the end of a shift. He was seated at the end of the pit on a dead game. He looked up and said, "I guess you know what this is."

I nodded.

He told me that the list of names came down from upstairs and that he had no say in it.

"They don't even have the balls to hand us the pink slips themselves," I said.

"Well, I got you out early," he said.

I took the slip and signed it. It was marked "eligible for rehire." I laughed and asked, "Is that so I won't take them to court?"

The shift boss shook his head. I left.

Within two weeks, we had been replaced, most of us by young women. Because many of us who were fired were in protected categories, two blacks and most over forty, we contacted an attorney. He listened and seemed interested in the case, but he needed money. Several of the dealers who'd been fired needed jobs right away and were afraid that suing would hurt their chances for employment elsewhere. The idea of the suit died between Christmas and New Year's. But that's not the whole story.

A day or so after we were fired, the same managers who'd fired us hired a temporary Santa Claus who'd been terminated from his seasonal job at the Boulevard Mall for being drunk on the job. This same Santa wore a red and white uniform and hung around the lounge at the Maxim, passing out piddling trinkets to guests from a big red gift bag.

The newspapers wrote a human interest story that made the management at the Maxim sound like humanitarians. Four of us used our gift certificates and went to eat at Da Vinci's. Afterward we went to the lounge to have a drink. There was Santa, half-snockered, greeting people with a handshake and a little wrapped gift. Someone recognized us as we sat sipping our after-dinner drinks. A security guard approached us and said that as soon as we finished our drinks, we were to leave.

There's still more. Art Woods was the general manager. When he died of emphysema and bitterness a few years later, I called up one of the dealers who'd been fired at the same time, and we toasted the selfish old toad. We both had better jobs because we'd been fired. Sometime after that, one of the other management decision makers died in a motorcycle crash in Utah. The papers said he was a good family man. So were many of the people he'd fired without cause. None of us mourned either of them. The Maxim has never recovered from the management policies of that period. It has filed for bankruptcy and gone into receivership at least once, and now the casino is entirely closed, just a shell of a place off the Strip, part of the ever-changing skyline. If casinos can be haunted, you can bet that place is.

It was a long time ago, but the memory of it stings even now. No matter whether you're a player or a dealer, the odds are always in the house's favor.

UNDATED

It's all a matter of record. Jack Trenkle was the casino manager at the Showboat then. He was old school. One day this woman employee comes up to him and asks for an extra day off. He tells her that her tits aren't big enough, just like that. Well, she said something to someone. Jack drew some heat. I guess he was told to cool it, but it didn't end there.

There was this woman on the floor. She'd been dealing for quite a while but had been promoted. Her name was Boom Boom. I swear. Like I said, it's a matter of record. She was a pretty busty woman. She's dead now, I think. Anyhow, anyone with any sense isn't going to cross a woman named Boom Boom. Anyone, that is, but Jack Trenkle. I can't remember what it was exactly that she wanted—change days off, maybe an extra day off, but Jack hit her with the same kind of remark about her breasts. You'd think he'd learn.

She sued. Went first to the Labor Relations Board and filed a complaint, got it down on record. The case was settled before it went to trial. I don't know how much she got. A sizeable amount, though, to be sure. As for Jack, last thing I heard he was working the eye in the sky somewhere. Like a lot of those old-time bosses, he couldn't make the adjustment to the way the world is now.

1989

I'm a Jew. It's a fact. My mother and father were Jews, so it follows, I guess, that I'm one. I don't practice my faith. In that way, I'm wrong. But I believe in the Jews' basic beliefs, and I believe Jews must look out for one another. And I believe Jews, above everything else, must have a sense of humor. I see nothing wrong with this and will not apologize for feeling that way. I also believe Jews should never harm those who are not Jews. Live and let live, that's how I believe. Not all Jews feel as I do, but most would tell you all Jews are brothers in the eyes of God.

When I began on the Strip, I worked for Carl Cohen. He was a Jew and a good man. So were Harry Goodhart and Al Benedict. The Sands was small, especially by today's standards. It was more than a place to earn money, although we did that, and no one resented a penny we made. Harry especially would stop and ask how you were doing, ask after your children by name. Family is important to everyone, but to a Jew, family is everything. I have Cuban and Italian friends who are the same. So maybe we were spoiled. But we were good to the customers in those days. People would bring me onion bagels from New York, in big brown bags, and I would share them with my friends at work. We got along well. Maybe it's because the prosperity was passed around. No one argued.

Carl was a tough man when he had to be. He's the one who punched Frank Sinatra and broke his caps. That's because Sinatra threatened him with his connections. I don't know if Carl and Al were connected. People said they were. I believed it, but I didn't know. It wasn't important. Like I said, they were good men and good to me. "How's the boys?" they would ask. And that made me feel good.

So, years later, long after Carl's dead and Al was still alive and at the MGM and Harry was running the Desert Inn, things changed overnight. The new regime was headed by . . . I won't even say his name. He, like me, was a Jew, but he wasn't like me or Harry or Al or Carl. He came in like he was ready to set fire to us. You could see by the way he looked at people that he hated them. Me, I like people. It's important to like them and let them know it. You say hello and goodbye and how are you and how are your children. You say these things because every human life is important. I believe this, just as I believe Jews must regard one another as blood. You see, we are always one step away from the Holocaust. Every Jew lost someone in concentration camps. To think otherwise is sinful. Cousins, great aunts, maybe mothers or fathers or friends of mothers or fathers. My father used to tell stories of an uncle who died, but the stories were of him as a young man who was courting a rich man's daughter. But it was like I knew this uncle. And it made me sad that he died. He was a man with heart, a real *mensch,* my father would say.

Almost the first day this new boss takes over, the atmosphere changes. He tells players who've been coming for twenty years that their old credit line is no good, that they must fill out new applications and be approved. A woman who lost ten thousand was handed a bill in the coffee shop and signed it. She had lost hundreds of thousands over the years. She was asked to pay for a Danish and coffee. Dealers on a dead game were no longer allowed to look about. Bosses were not allowed to talk to dealers about anything except to correct them. The list went on and on. One day he threw a party for a blackjack tournament and had a violinist play in the pit as he sang "I Left My Heart in San Francisco" to the players. He had a strong accent, the heavy German kind. He gave orders that dealers could not get tips from the players in the tournament. It began his reign of terror.

We found out he had a limited license and wasn't supposed to involve himself directly in the casino operation, but he did. One day a dealer said hello to him. He sent a boss over to the table later to tell the dealer never to do that again. So word comes around the pit that none of us, no dealer, is to look this new boss in the face. If one does, it's out the door for him. I was used to the old Sands. You fired yourself. Deal the game and be considerate of customers, and the job was yours until the heart attack. What kind of person tells others you can't look at me or else I'll punish you? What kind of man takes another man's dignity away? I'll tell you.

One day one of my friends, a man I've known twenty years, tells me of this new boss, whose name I cannot bear to say. He tells me this man lost his father in a concentration camp. I said that I heard the same thing.

"Oh, yeah," my friend said. "Bet you don't know how."

"How?" I ask.

"He fell out of a guard tower."

I laughed. I not only laughed, I repeated the story to others, even to my wife and sons. I knew I should be ashamed, being Jewish, you understand. The Holocaust is nothing to ever joke about. But I wasn't ashamed because the man who tells another "I'll punish you for looking at me" is the same as a Nazi. What other kind of man would make such a terrible rule? Isn't this a free country? I know a good man when I meet one. Harry and Al and Carl were good men and good bosses to work for. They were good Jews. They would never do something so rotten to another human being. I know I was wrong to laugh in some people's eyes. But what good has a Jew done who attacks the rights of other men?

1980

I went to work my first night at Vegas World ready to do the right thing. You understand, make a good impression. I was hired as a floorman. Now they have titles like "game supervisor" and such. But it's the same thing—the lowest level of casino management. I was wearing an expensive suit, too expensive for the joint, a shiny Italian silk suit. Anyhow, I walk in the pit, which is busy as hell with all kinds of people, mostly budget-tourist types. As I walk in the pit I see this guy in slacks and a sports shirt lying on top of a blackjack table, and he smells of alcohol.

Right away I know I'm not working in the average casino. I mean, every place I'd ever worked in would have rolled this guy out of the front door onto the sidewalk. But here, no one's paying a bit of attention. There are bosses just a few feet away, and they're just ignoring the problem. As I said, it's my first night, and I want to make an impression, so I walk to the nearest podium in the pit and pick up the phone and ask for security. I'm going to tell them about the drunk passed out on the table.

As I'm dialing, the pitboss strolls over and asks who I am. We don't know each other. I tell him I'm the new floor boss for craps. He nods. I nod. Then I tell the operator I want security to get a drunk off a blackjack game. The pitboss shakes his head and tells me to hang up. I do, but naturally I'm confused. He pulls me aside and tells me not to worry about the stiff on the table, that it's only Bob Stupak and that in a little while security will come by and take him up to a room. I nodded and asked where I was assigned. I knew I had to modify some of my thinking about how casinos should be run.

Stupak was the owner. In that sense it was his table. Who was I to tell him where or where not to pass out? I signed my name on the sign-in sheet and followed the pitboss to the craps pit, where I was introduced around. No one mentioned the incident with Stupak. Business as usual, you might say.

1969

When he was GM at the Riviera, Ed Torres, known for his temperament, walked into the craps pit late in the shift. It was a busy night, and he was in a hurry carrying a handful of papers and wasn't looking where he was going. He was noted for being preoccupied, and that's being kind. As he entered, he stepped into a stand used by the shorter dealers so they can reach around the layout. He lost his balance, stumbled, and fell face down, his papers settling down beside him. Everyone laughed. It was kind of funny, almost like a skit, but he didn't think so. He got up red-faced and burning to retaliate. But who could he retaliate against? It was an accident.

He asked the pitboss what the hell the stand was doing in the pit, never mind that a dealer was standing on it at the time.

"The short dealers use them to stand on," the pitboss said.

"Yeah, well, get rid of them. I won't have them."

"But what will my dealers stand on?"

Torres thought a moment and said, "Fire the short dealers."

"But you can't just do that," the pitboss said. "We'll be sued, and half the dealers are short."

Torres looked around, thinking and studying what he saw—the stand, the dealers, the tables. Finally he said, "Cut four inches off the legs of the craps tables."

"Cut the legs off?"

"Yes."

"What will my other dealers do? The tall ones?"

Torres didn't blink. "I don't care, and if they complain, fire them." He stormed out of the pit, was gone a few minutes, then returned for his papers. Everyone got another laugh in, but the next day when they came to work, the craps dealers were dealing on tables that were four inches shorter.

1988

You hear how much they regard you as an employee, how you're part of a team, all that stuff. In some ways you want to believe it, but it's hard not to get cynical. We had a new administration at the Sands. They said that things were going to change, and the way it was said it sounded more like a threat than a grand plan. And it was true that things changed. Our income dropped by some 25 percent, and some of us had to go on a four-day work schedule, which knocked out another 20 percent or so. Buses parked at the south entrance, and retirees brought their coupons to the tables to play. They had mugs in their hands filled with coupons, two-for-one payoffs on bets, a dollar's worth of nickels good at the slot department, a free buffet for two. The management was right: Things changed. At the same time, working conditions got worse. The dealers were treated like we were ungrateful plantation slaves (an exaggeration because we were actually viewed as plantation slaves without the cruel physical treatment).

In the midst of all this "change" a rumor started that one day someone had called in a bomb threat. Who knows where the rumor came from? Supposedly, security passed the information on to the executives. In the story, the suits told security not to call the police or fire department, then the executives evacuated the offices and headed for safer territory. The dealers, first-line management, restaurant help, and other casino workers were never notified. They just kept pumping cards to the little ladies from Riverside. The rumor pointed to the general manager as the one who'd made the decision not to inform the help. Even as the story grew and circulated, it became fact. No one questioned it.

One dealer said the general manager probably thought a dealer called the threat in to get an extra break. We thought the remark was pretty humorous until someone asked, "What if there had been a bomb?" I think it was Tony who said, "The survivors would have to deal to the survivors." I have no idea if the incident happened, or if something similar prompted the rumor, or if it was started out of boredom or out of maliciousness. What's telling from all of this is how quickly we dealers bought into the rumor. It was obvious that the new management was looking down their noses at us, so the bomb story confirmed in extreme terms what we believed they'd do under any circumstance—leave us out to hang.

Whenever anyone in a casino talks to me about team spirit and all that now, I just smile and nod and go on with what I'm paid to do, nothing more, nothing less. It's hard not to be a cynic, very hard. And it's just as hard not to believe rumors.

1980

I'll never forget the day. November 21. It's over twenty years ago, isn't it? I've worked in casinos twenty-six years now. I finally had a good job. It wasn't Caesars, but the money was good. I had two kids and no husband, and I was catching up on my bills. I'd been at the MGM about a year, no, a little over that, fifteen months. I'd made a few friends there, just to get along mostly. My daughters were my life. If you work with people daily, like we do in casinos, it's best not to let them know your business. In that way, I was different than most of the women dealers. Looking back, I'm glad. It was devastating enough to go through what we went through that day. Hell, that week.

I smelled something burning long before anyone was alarmed about the fire. You could smell it when walking to and from the dealers' room. We worked for a guy named Vic Wakeman. He was a dwarf, and we called him "The Eye in the Carpet," a play on "the eye in the sky," the people who watch the action from above. Someone said something about Vic being up in the eye and probably burning up because some high roller had made a score the night before. I worked graveyard shift. Most of the dealers were half asleep. I went back on my blackjack game at twenty 'til seven. I even mentioned the smell to my floorman. He shrugged and said something about security would be on it if there was a fire and that it was probably just some trash can that caught fire when someone put a cigarette in it. I had two players on my game, so I started pumping cards. People who play at six and seven o'clock in the morning are serious players.

I've thought about how much more serious it might have been if the fire had hit on swing shift or early graveyard. The panic and everything would have cost a lot more lives on the casino floor. As it was, we were lucky. When it hit, when the ceiling began to collapse and the flames sprouted at the far end of the casino near the restaurant, no one was overly alarmed. My floorman told the players we would have to shut down the game for a few minutes. Why upset a player? They didn't want to leave. He told me to bring up my lid and started to count down the rack before he locked the bank. I looked to my left and shook my head.

"We gotta go," I said.

The smoke was so thick fifty feet away I could barely see. You could feel the fire when the first flames shot through the smoke. I backed away from the table and took off. My floorman did the same. I passed tables where dealers and floor supervisors were locking up games. You could see that the dealers were scared. I told a couple of them to forget it and hit the door. Despite the confusion, the lack of any plan, or someone taking charge, we left in a surprisingly orderly way. Dealers and security and supervisors let customers get out first. A moment after we'd made it out of the casino, a second ball of flame exploded by the door.

It may sound selfish, but as the smoke started to swallow the casino and crawl up the outside walls, I stood there wondering what I was going to do for a job. I had my girls. They wouldn't understand. The first firemen were there by then. I can only imagine what they were thinking when they saw the smoke. They had to feel like ants trying to bring down an elephant. I hurried to the parking lot. My babysitter would be dressing the girls for school by then. I didn't hang around. I wanted to go home to my girls and hold them. One was in fourth grade, the other in second. I wanted them to know their mommy was all right. I didn't want them to hear about it at school. That's selfish, I know, but that was what was on my mind. I guess I was kind of in shock. I figure I am alive now by two or three minutes at best.

What were there, seventy people killed, seventy-five [eighty-five fatalities]? Some were employees. I knew a few of them. I was glad I'd kept to myself. I wasn't close to anyone, so the sense of loss wasn't the same for me as others. I got calls later, mostly the next day. All sorts of rumors from other dealers. No one really knew anything, but they believed everything. Some of them were devastated. I can understand. I kept my girls out of school. I fixed their meals and sat with them, reading or watching TV most of the day. We all got under a blanket and snuggled. Sometimes I'd cry, sniffle really. They asked me what was wrong. I'd ask if they were hungry and go get some doughnuts or graham crackers. I couldn't tell them what was wrong.

I got another job right before the new year. Christmas was a little scant that year, but I spent it with the girls, the whole day, popping popcorn and listening to Christmas carols. I was damned near broke, but it was the happiest Christmas I ever had. I remember it now almost as clearly as I remember the fire. My parents kicked in a few extra presents. We opened packages on Christmas Eve. I didn't string up lights on the tree, just ornaments. I was scared as hell of fire. I took pictures of my girls. They were so cute. They're both married now. I'm a grandmother twice. I think of the people who died, the ones I knew, and I can't find their faces anywhere. It's sad. I was lucky. Some others weren't.

1970s

I was at the Stardust when Glick brought in Lefty Rosenthal to run things. Glick was the front man, and Maury Aaronberg was the casino manager, but everyone knew Rosenthal was running the show. Baccarat was a cash game then. Rosenthal stood around in the pit like he owned the place, and maybe with Tony the Ant and the Chicago Boys backing him, it was the same as being the owner. I heard that a lot of money never saw the count room. Believe it.

The Stardust had always been a Mob joint, but it was a good store. We made a decent living and worked for some real characters. Guys like Al Facinto and Al Sachs. They didn't bother you. Besides, everyone on the Strip was juiced in those days. Everyone had a relative or friend who was in some way connected—marriage or went to school with someone who was in. It wasn't any big deal. Either that or you were just a regular guy and someone liked you. Of course, you had to deal.

The Stardust was a major grind joint. Before the show and a show break, you couldn't move in the aisles. The Lido brought them in like no other show in town. Busy, that's what it was. It wasn't a bad gig, just a lot of humping behind the table and no one riding your ass.

That's before Lefty.

I remember when he first started there. He was tall and skinny and pale like an albino, kind of sickly looking, if you ask me. Someone told me he was some big Mob guy, but it was hard to believe when you saw him—couldn't beat Phyllis Diller at arm wrestling with the help of Charles Atlas. He walked around in expensive Italian silk suits, all tailor-made, his bug eyes looking half-asleep, half-bored, never blinking—cold eyes, eyes like he could eat a fudge brownie and choke his grandmother at the same time. I'll tell you one thing, he was no muscle, but he was mean and cold as one. The man must have been hollow inside. It took about three days and three hours for him to earn every dealer's scorn. We called him The Ostrich.

I saw the movie *Casino* and nearly choked. De Niro played the Rosenthal character. He was supposed to be some kind of genius, right? He was a bookie, a handicapper, who'd fixed college games. He knew nothing about what happens in a casino, but he was there to guarantee the skim. Next thing you know, he's calling all the shots. Who gets hired. Who gets fired. I don't know if he ever saw a damned game. He walked around looking at the toes of his shoes. Or stood and did the same, even when he was talking to someone. I don't think he ever looked a dealer in the eye, at least not a male dealer.

Next thing you know, the male blackjack dealers are getting axed and replaced by women dealers. When he came there we had three women dealers. Within six months we had a pit full of them, most all of them from the Golden Nugget and good looking or so stacked it didn't matter if their faces looked like Lon Chaney as the werewolf. I've got nothing against women—like them, in fact—but that was wrong firing us and hiring them. Before you go thinking Rosenthal was trying to even the playing field or was interested in advancing affirmative action, let me set the record straight. Here was his genius, his logic at work behind all the firings. He was a thief, and he was a man. The dealers at the Stardust were mostly males. Since he was male and a thief, it followed that we, too, must have been thieves. So he started firing us and hiring women, who naturally weren't men and, therefore, not thieves. That, my friend, is the logic of the casinos when the Mob ran them, at least when paranoiacs like Rosenthal ran them. But, hey, the logic of casino management makes even less sense now that corporations run them. On the other hand, Rosenthal never was lonely with all those women playing up to him.

I worked at one place where they gave us pep talks every other week, like we were Japanese factory workers or insurance salesmen. And they still fired us for some pretty stupid reasons. One guy I worked with was terminated for not smiling. He wasn't rude, just didn't smile. He even went through a personnel hearing before he was let go. There were no customer complaints against him, just two warning slips from the same boss saying he didn't smile. He'd worked for the same casino eleven years, hadn't smiled for eleven years, and hadn't pissed anyone off. The corporate suits wanted us all to act like greeters at Disneyland. Being a good dealer isn't enough anymore. You have to look like a numbskull on Prozac to survive in a casino. Could be Rosenthal's logic makes better sense.

I was one of the dealers Rosenthal fired without cause. Don't know how he picked me out. Maybe he saw my reflection in the toes of his shoes. Anything was possible with him. He survived that bombing in the Tony Roma parking lot on Sahara. Man, that was a disappointment. If you ask me, the guy who blew that job should've been fitted for cement shoes. More than one dealer thought that way. It's cold, I know, but some homicides are commendable. I understand Lefty's still alive, owns a restaurant down in Florida or something like that. Too bad. I don't mean about the restaurant. I hear he wants to be called Frank, that he hates the name Lefty. Well, if you happen to bump into him, tell him, "Hi, Lefty." Tell him I hear ostriches can be mean, too.

1980s

We were fired from the Hilton over a period of a few months, about eighty of us, given termination slips that said, "Change of personnel." Most of us had been there since the place opened as the International. Many of us had worked for Kerkorian at the Flamingo. We were forty or older when they decided to put us out the door. Well, we decided to sue. Now, that in itself was kind of a new idea, and scary. The gaming industry operates with impunity. It controls the state. The casinos contribute to both sides in an election, so that no matter who wins, an obligation follows. I have friends who are from Montana, and they tell me that's how it was when Anaconda Copper was the big industry in Butte, and Anaconda was owned by Standard Oil. The mining company owned the legislature and the judges. I've seen dealers blackballed. That's was what we were risking by suing.

When it came down to push and shove, we figured it was just our turn for a change. Casinos had been getting by with firing people en masse for years, except for the culinary help, because they had a union. A new general manager would take over a place and bring in a new casino manager, who would bring in his pitbosses and dealers. The old employees were fired, no warning, no reason. Well, this time the Hilton messed up. The management hired mostly younger women to take our places. The pattern was set.

We filed discrimination complaints with the Equal Employment Opportunity Commission. We had obviously been discriminated against. Since we were male and all white, the EEOC didn't do anything. They gave us lip service, but ultimately nothing else. The message was essentially that we weren't protected by the same regulations that protect women and minorities. I guess they hated the idea of us using the laws that were intended for a select group. Don't get me wrong, I think minorities got a raw deal and still do, but damn it, discrimination is discrimination no matter who's doing it and who's on the receiving end. We were mad. Once the EEOC failed to act on our complaints, the groundwork was set for a suit, and we filed a class action suit against the Hilton asking for reimbursement of lost wages and reinstatement to our positions.

The grind began. Years. It wasn't easy. Some of us had to take jobs for less money or jobs outside of gaming. The Hilton's strategy was to delay the case as long as possible, appeal after appeal. A few, though we couldn't prove it, were blackballed. Some of us lost families, some lost their health, some of us lost heart, a couple became alcoholics, and others died. Every time we'd win on appeal and think the case was about to go to court, there'd be another appeal. It was a circus, almost laughable. Attorneys representing the Hilton knew their defense wouldn't hold up in front of a jury, so they kept demanding a trial by a judge, one thing after another.

Years went by. We won in 1987. Then we lost most of the money on an appeal. We got the short end, all of us. Eventually I ended up with

$32,000, which is a little less than what I would have netted in a year dealing at the Hilton. It's a new century, and I never got my job back. You win, but you lose. I understand the Hilton was a great place to work for many years after we filed the suit. The dealers were treated exceptionally well until just recently. I don't know for sure, but that's what I heard. I'll say one thing about it: You won't see mass firings in this business any more, not unless the economy goes bad and the casinos legitimately have to lay off help. Well, maybe that's mostly hope talking.

Was it worth it? I'd like to say it was, but the truth is we didn't have a choice. It was go to court or roll over. Some people tell me to be thankful for what I ended up with. I lost my job, a lot of money, some property, and a wife. Who do I thank for all that? That's what I want to know. Just who the hell should I thank?

1969

Years ago, when I'd been at the Stardust a couple of years, Bobby Stella, the casino manager, put his brother-in-law, who'd been out of work, to work as a dealer. The guy had been a mechanic or something before and not the swiftest sail on the sea. The brother-in-law may as well have had five thumbs on each hand. I guess the sister and brother-in-law were buried and no work, kids and all that, too. Well, Bobby was a typical kind of Italian when it came to family and pretty generous with others as well, but he put himself up against it with this relative.

Nepotism was the order of the day back then. No one thought a thing of it. The Stardust was full of all sorts of characters in those days, and more than a few of them were working because they were related to the bosses. You earned, between the tips and the wages, about fifty-five or sixty-five a day, and no one was paying taxes on the tips, and a house cost less than thirty thousand. A lot of people moved here and called on family ties to get work. Hell, I did the same thing, but I learned how to deal.

Like I said, we weren't getting rich off tips, but the joint was steady, and our envelopes contained just under forty a day, day in, day out, unless we had a big George in, meaning a high roller who toked heavy.

The brother-in-law was an all-right kind of guy in some ways but would pick up his envelope at the beginning of the shift and on his breaks give the money to a keno runner to play keno for him. Before the shift was over each day, the brother-in-law was broke. This went on for months. Then when Bobby found out the guy was burying his sister and family even deeper, he fired him. Bobby said it was the only way he knew that he could put food on his sister's table.

I don't know where the brother-in-law ended up, but I'm pretty sure he didn't stay with dealing. He may have left town. Who knows? I remember we all got a big chuckle out of that story.

1984

A friend of mine set me up to see the casino manager at the Aladdin. The manager's name was Tony. I didn't know him, but my buddy was supposed to be tight with someone. We're all easterners, Jersey and New York, and everyone knows someone. So I'm supposed to be juiced in. I show up and page this Tony. He tells me to meet him by the craps pit.

He's waiting when I get there, his arms folded over his chest. I tell him very politely that my friend sent me to ask about a job and that I wanted to put in an application and have an audition. I mention my friend's name. Tony doesn't flinch. He says, "I don't know no buddy of yours. I don't know you. And I ain't got no job openings for no dealers. Come see me after six months." He walks away.

I was humiliated. I figured my buddy set me up, but I didn't say anything to him because I didn't want to let on that I'd been had. A few days later my buddy calls and asks how the job thing went. Well, I proceed to give him hell for setting me up. He slows me down, says there's been a mistake and convinces me to go back. I'm in no hurry to be had again, but I agree to go. Now, in the meantime, about ten days have gone by. I show up and ask for Tony. This time he meets me and shakes my hand, says he's been waiting for me for several days, then he walks me into his office and has me sit down. He asks if I want some coffee, talks to me like we played marbles together in grade school. I tell him I want to call my buddy and thank him, but Tony says it's not necessary, that all the thanks have been taken care of.

1972

Major Riddle was about the strangest man I'd ever seen in the casino business—and that covers a lot of territory. He was kind of proof that you only needed money to make it good. We'd watch him play poker in the poker pit at the Dunes. He was on the license but could play poker because the house didn't bank the play. You know, player against player, supposedly. One Saturday night Riddle (already an old man) was in the poker room playing against a guy named Billy Douglas, who was a card cheater and a hell of a poker player with or without cheating. There were two other pros playing on the same table. I knew Billy. He was a damn fine paint man, very skilled at marking a deck. He could work up a deck and read the cards as well as anyone. Got himself killed back in the early seventies, went to Kentucky, I think it was, and worked up a deck against two hillbilly brothers who didn't take kindly to being taken. But neither Billy nor the others tampered with the deck when Riddle was in action. They didn't have to.

Everyone in the joint from Abe Schiller all the way to the casino porter knew that Riddle was getting hustled, that the best he had going for him was to play the best of the three hands every time. To keep him going, the three players would let Riddle win the small pots. It was ego. The Major would rake the chips in and sneer like he was one stud poker player. It was slow that night, and I was standing on a dead game clocking the action because I had nothing better to do. Here I am working, in a sense, for this millionaire and wondering just how the hell he got his money.

Before the shift was out, the Major had lost about twenty thousand. A security guard walked him up to his room. Billy Douglas and the other characters cashed in their winnings. They split everything three ways, didn't even try to hide the fact, just cut the money up at the cashier cage in front of everybody.

At the time Riddle owned the Silver Nugget, a downscale joint in North Vegas. I heard a couple of nights later how he was telling another boss about a dealer at the Silver Nugget passing off five-dollar chips to a girlfriend. The dealer had been under suspicion for a while, and the Major wanted to be there to see the man arrested. When the bust went down, Riddle was in the eye in the sky watching the action. He said he wanted to jump right through the two-way mirror and beat the man with his cane. Riddle had the man arrested and brought to the security office in handcuffs. He said it took three security guards and a couple of gaming agents to pull him off the dealer, that he could have killed him, he was so mad. He was genuinely outraged that anyone would steal from him. That night he went back to the poker table and sat down with Billy Douglas and his cronies and got taken to the cleaners again. The Major was a shrewd character, a real genius, proof that if you've got the money, you don't have to have a brain in your skull.

1976

The Horseshoe kept its big-six game at the entrance. One day shift, a break-in was dealing the game. She'd probably been in the business around two months. Behind the big-six was the bird game, a twenty-five-cent-minimum craps game. The bird game had a few regulars playing on it. The floorman on that game and the boss in the craps pit were supposed to keep an eye on the big-six. It was slow. No one was really paying much attention to anything, much less the big-six, when all of a sudden some tourist lands on the game and buys in for forty dollars and starts betting the twenty- and forty-to-ones.

Of course, the dealer calls out that money is in action, and neither the floorman nor the pitboss is paying attention. The bank on the big-six held about four hundred in chips of various amounts from twenty-five cents to twenty-five dollars. The guy hit a few, and before the bosses realized why the dealer was raising such a racket, the rack in front of her was empty. The boss ordered a fill. The player had to wait for it. A boss was assigned to watch the game. The dealer kept spinning, and the player kept winning and tipping. No matter how the dealer spun the wheel, she could not win. She switched sides. She spun fast. She spun slow. The wheel came to rest on the twenty- and forty-to-one so regularly that five more fills were brought to the game, and the player was by then betting twenty-five-dollar checks. He won so much that two bosses were assigned to the game, and Ted Binion was called.

Before the player cashed out, he had hit the Horseshoe for more than ten thousand dollars. He tipped the dealer, all totaled, fifteen hundred dollars, which was a fairly substantial amount. Ted Binion arrived toward the end of the action. He refused to believe that anyone could win that much money on the big-six without help. He suspected not only the dealer but also the floorman and fired them both. Still not satisfied, he got the dealers responsible for cutting tokes off their games and had them open the toke box that the fifteen hundred in tips had been dropped in.

Ted Binion took that fifteen hundred and put it back in the rack on the big-six, which was a violation of gaming regulations and, if you could get anyone to file charges, theft. Once that money went in the box, it belonged to the dealers. But this was the Horseshoe, and who was going to complain?

1978?

In those days we used to work six days a week at the Showboat. This one kid was getting married, and he went up to Pete Amante, who ran the schedule, and told him that he was getting married and needed three days off. When the next schedule came out, Pete had given the kid three days off—Monday, Wednesday, and Friday.

1970

In the late sixties and early seventies the Riv—that's what we called the Riviera—was a good joint. In its heyday it was a classy place. The male gamblers would show up in suit and tie, and the ladies dressed to the nines. We all made money. A few high rollers provided the seasoning, and we had headliner entertainment in the showroom to put the meat and gravy on the table. Shecky Green and others filled the casino with patrons. The show lines strung out from the showroom to the hotel lobby and out the south entrance. That was a couple of hundred yards. Security guards hustled customers from the back of the line to the front for about five bucks a head. One old guard named Lou probably knocked down a hundred a night hustling. The wait was so long that some gamblers would have a wife or girlfriend hold his place in line while he made a quick lay-down. And they tipped when they won. A few stiffs, but mostly not.

We dealers were pocketing a buck to a buck twenty-five [$100–$125] a shift on week days and double that on weekends. I used to burn rubber to San Diego on my days off and stay at the Hotel del

Coronado on Coronado Island. I had money to blow. I'd take my wife. I'd surf fish in the daytime, and at night we'd go dancing somewhere or just walk the beach. She worked cocktails at the Frontier. Between us, we made a nice living. We took vacations to Hawaii and the Caribbean and once to Europe, France and Italy. It was sweet. The Riv was a good cow to milk.

But it was a tough place to work, especially for a Mob joint. Every dealer behind a table had juice of some kind or was such a crackerjack clerk that the bosses were just happy to have him working the game. No women then. They worked cocktails or carried a tray full of cigarettes and cigars. We knew that the top bosses were skimming and the money was going back to the Midwest. Some of the best high rollers we dealt to were Teamsters officials. I heard it was Teamsters money and Mob muscle that kept the carpet on the floor. We weren't allowed to talk to players unless it concerned something like one wanting cocktails or cigarettes. The bosses were afraid we'd give up help to them. Some of the customers were lame, couldn't play basic strategy, but it didn't matter. The Mob boys were greedy that way. Besides, I don't think Ed Torres [the general manager] trusted anyone. I think he thought all of us were crooks. In those days the only ones allowed to steal were the top bosses and those dealers who helped with scams. And there were plenty of them going down. I'm not at liberty to discuss any I know about. Some of the people I worked with are still around, and some of them work with me now.

We all knew Ed Torres got his position because he was connected. He was a strange guy. I worked there seven years. I don't think he ever talked to me except once or twice to say hello. I remember he used to talk to a cocktail waitress on our shift, to her and the cigarette girl. The cigarette girl had one of those personalities, bubbly and quick witted. She was going to the university. I think she graduated. Anyhow, Ed just wasn't a friendly guy with the help. What always amazed me was seeing Ed Torres early in the morning when the casino was slow. Here's this guy knocking down the big money, and he'd sit on a dead game as if he were thinking of something pretty important, but as soon as someone got up and left a game empty and the ashtray was dirty, Mr. Torres would walk over and empty it. That was the casino porter's job. We used to joke about Ed Torres being the highest-paid porter on the Strip.

When he bought the Silverbird, which had been the old Thunderbird, he built a new casino. It went belly up. I can't remember all the

circumstances, but I remember it being dark and abandoned and thinking what a waste. Maybe someone who did something besides empty-
ing ashtrays could have made the place go. I think it went into bankruptcy and receivership. I wasn't surprised. I don't think anyone who
worked for Torres at the Riviera expected anything different.

This kid worked baccarat at the same time I was there. His old man
was a shylock, an Italian who was supposed to be pretty well connected, not a made guy, I don't think, but mobbed up. Anyhow, this kid
was nineteen years old, just graduated high school. He looked older,
not by much. Now, I'm guessing because I never worked the baccarat
pit, but I'd heard some figures, and I figure the kid is making sixty to
seventy grand a year. Nineteen years old! Juice, the kid had it big.

One night some vice detectives pull him out of the game, this kid.
They ask for his ID, and the next thing you know the kid's in handcuffs.
Right there on the casino floor. I watched it all go down. Now out of
nowhere, the shift boss, who was Torres's main man, beelines it for the
pit. I guess the pitboss in baccarat called him down. The detective who
seemed to be running the show was young himself, early twenties
maybe. He was doing his job. The minimum age for gambling or even
being in a casino is twenty-one. Can't blame the cop for doing his job.
Both the kid and the casino were in clear violation of the law. But there
was the shift boss talking his head off, trying to talk that young detective out of doing his job.

I was never much of one for cops, didn't have anything against
them, mind you, but nothing for them, either. But I sure admired that
young cop. He was this blond-headed kid, and it was easy to see he
wasn't intimidated in the least. I heard him say the kid who was in
handcuffs was going to jail and so was anyone who tried to interfere.
The shift boss said he wanted to talk to the detective's supervisor, and I
heard the cop say, "Talk to him all you want, but get out of my way."

The next night, the kid was back in the baccarat pit making his
nightly cut of seventy thousand a year. He was never arrested again
that I know of, and I never saw that young detective after that. Juice,
that was how it worked. I bet Ed Torres made the call that sprung the
kid, and I'll bet he was hooked into some judge or was owed a political
favor. The joints contributed to a lot of political campaigns then. The
cop was right doing what he did. I've got nothing against that kid who
was dealing, but right's right and wrong's wrong, isn't it? I watched
those two detectives march off with that kid, and I thought, all right.

1980

In December my townhouse caught fire, and the upstairs was destroyed while I was at work. Among the items lost in the fire were all of my military records, books, pictures from my childhood, letters, drapes, blinds, two bedrooms of furniture, a television, and all my clothing. My roommate and I had to stay with my sister and brother-in-law for a week. The insurance covered the repair of the structure. All else was a total loss.

My brother-in-law purchased two changes of work clothes and a pair of jeans for me, as my checkbook was also gone. I went to work the next day. That evening I was on the big-six game. It was slow, and I had no customers. The casino manager came over and said he'd heard that my place had burned down. I said that was true, that I lost all my personal papers and photos and everything in my closet.

"Well," he said, "consider it a liberating experience."

At first I was stunned. I expected nothing from him anyhow, then I stared at him and nodded slowly.

"Sure. That's how I'll view death as well."

He smiled and walked away.

5

CHEATING

Wherever a commodity can be converted easily into cash, thieves will prosper. Over the years, casinos, with their huge money banks and millions of dollars' worth of chips, have been havens for all manner of cheats. The skimming scams of the seventies—especially at the Stardust, the Tropicana, and the Dunes—are a part of the Las Vegas Mob history. Millions were "raked off the top" by organized crime front men. The slot manager at the Stardust disappeared shortly before a multimillion-dollar skimming operation was uncovered. One dealer said that if he had a choice between taking the profits or what was stolen out of Caesars Palace in his twenty-six years of working there, it would be a hard decision to make. But either way, he would be a very rich man.

All that money "back doored," and the casinos still prosper!

Although under constant observation, dealers have managed to rake off their share as well, some of it from their fellow employees. No one is more despised by dealers than the thief who steals tips, yet ironically these are the dealers who walk out the front door of one casino and into the back door of another with seeming impunity. Part of the problem is that casinos don't want to intervene or take any responsibility for dealers' tips. If the thief hasn't stolen from the joint, the casinos don't prosecute. At the Mint in the late seventies a dealer who cut tips (the general manager's nephew) embezzled an average of over five hundred a night from his fellow dealers—a figure modestly estimated based on the fact that after he was caught, tips went up an average of twelve dollars per dealer per day. What finally led to his downfall was his own greed. He'd been stealing before the shift's final take was counted and exchanged for cash, but one Saturday night (the big night for tokes) he returned and siphoned a couple of thousand more, took envelopes that had been sealed and blew the whole amount playing craps at the Horseshoe next door. He'd been doing this for months, and no one had mentioned his obvious habit, one that a downtown dealer could ill afford. He was never prosecuted. Later the dealers discovered he was the nephew of one of the top executives.

During the early seventies one of the cleverest cheating scams ever to infest the casinos involved dealers up and down the Strip and two groups who were competing for the action. The scam involved using a cylinder with a five-dollar chip on the top and the side painted to look like the edges of three more five-dollar chips (a stack of four reds). The outside man would simply bet the cylinder, which looked (even up close) just like a twenty-dollar bet. The dealer paid the bet if the player won or scooped the cylinder into the rack if the player lost. The dealer would then place the cylinder in the bank for the twenty-five-dollar chips, fill the cylinder with three twenty-five-dollar chips, and then, when the player won the next bet, pay him off with the cylinder, which contained the greens. The scam was uncovered when a hustler named Murphy was shot and killed by a rival gang for cutting into the action. Rumor had it that Johnny Hicks, a local kid who grew up in a rich family but wanted to be a gangster, was involved with the rival group. A few years later he himself was killed, a homicide that has gone unsolved. Hicks, a friend of Ted Binion, who was himself a victim of foul play, had finally made it as a gangster.

One of the most successful moves that dealers have used to cheat the casinos is the "Vegas handoff," a pass-off of chips on a craps game from the dealer to an outside agent. It is nothing more than a variation of the sleight of hand used by a magician to take someone's watch. All it requires is practice, practice, practice. The other most common move used by dealers was on the blackjack game, where at one time dealers looked at their hole cards. It gave a decided advantage to a player to know what the dealer had underneath the up card. There are a dozen other ways to cheat if a blackjack dealer can hold the deck. One of the ways is to deal seconds. Another is to use the "bubble peek" or the "heel peek" to see what the top card is and signal in some subtle way to the player whether or not to take a hit. Some dealers mastered changing the hole card. All these moves are no more mysterious than manipulations mastered by magicians. One thing to keep in mind is that these same cheating moves were at one time used to cheat the customer as well. Contrary to popular belief, casinos no longer cheat customers. The numbers are built in. But to the mid-sixties (this is a dirty little secret), "houses" kept "whack-out dealers" on the payroll, and some craps crews intentionally used their skills to underpay players.

All that money, and it's never enough!

1971

I was dealing to a table of stiffs, except for one guy. This was at the old Landmark before it was torn down. The casino was small, eighteen blackjack games, as I recall, and that day we didn't have all of them open, and I had probably the only full table in the joint. This guy who was winning and tipping was old—well, old to me then—probably sixty. He had salt-and-pepper hair and tortoiseshell glasses. He looked like someone's grandpa, not the jolly kind, though. He was quiet, too, didn't want to draw attention to himself, and real polite. Every hand he had me out there on the edge of the circle, twenty-five to a hundred for himself and five to ten for me.

I loved it. He couldn't lose. It wasn't like I was running cold, but he couldn't lose, except the occasional bet or if I popped a snapper. He never lost a double down. The floorman behind me comes up and tells me to break the deck down more often. We were dealing single deck in those days, and this clown behind me figured the old guy was counting. So, less than halfway through the deck I went to shuffle. The other players started grumbling, but the old guy just put up a hundred-dollar bet and ten in front for me. I dealt. He won. And he kept winning.

When my relief came, I thanked the old guy and went on my break. As I was going out of the pit I happened to look back and saw something strange. I wasn't sure what it was, but the old man seemed to make an extra move when he went to pin his cards under the bet. Instead of going to the break room, I got the pitboss and said someone should watch the old guy from outside the pit. I mean, I was dealing to him and couldn't see anything, but something was up. The pitboss said he'd take a look and have the man in the eye check it out as well.

I went to the break room, and when my break was over, I headed for the pit. We had to walk this long hallway that went west down a shopping promenade to the coffee shop and swimming pool, so I was going back the other way. As I passed some slow customers, I caught sight of a disturbance. Here came three security guards dragging the old man, who'd gone completely limp like those war protesters did during Vietnam. The toes of his shoes were scraping along the carpet, but he was dead quiet. And his hair was no longer salt and pepper, but dark brown and wavy, and he was fifteen years younger. Following the guards was the pitboss, who was all smiles. He held up a toupee for me to see.

Later they pulled me off the game so some detectives could interview me—what made me suspicious, etc. I said it was just that no one could win that many hands and that I thought I saw something, but I couldn't explain what. Mostly, it was a hunch. They told me that the old man was a well-known cheater, and he had this elaborate device operated with rubber bands that ran up his arm and down his chest to his legs, and he could use it to change the card faster than the eye could see. He was mucking cards in and out, filling in his hand.

I was a hero for about a shift. To tell the truth, the dealers were a bit pissed off. Here we had a George who was going to make our tokes for the day, and I got him arrested. They laughed, but they were a bit pissed, too. Anyhow, the case never made it to court. I left the Landmark for greener pastures about two months after that. I had people take cheap shots at me on a game, but that's the only time a pro ever hit my game. He was good. It was blind luck that nailed him. I still am not sure what I saw, but I saw it all the same.

1985

The best ever were these Middle Easterners who worked the wheels. They learned their trade in Europe and the Middle East and could past-post a bet faster and cleaner than you could ever imagine. They got it down the same way that all past-posters do, distraction here and down on the number, but they were just that much better than the others I had seen.

The way we made them was an accident. I was about to pay the straight ups on number twenty-three when a player sitting on the inside part of the layout asked me if he was allowed to place a bet after the ball dropped. I had the payoff cut out and ready to push. I paused and asked if he was joking. He said that he wasn't. I told him absolutely not.

"Then why can he do it?" he said and pointed to a man at the end of the table (not the one who had hit the number I was about to pay).

The Middle Easterner started to argue but thought the better of it when the man kept saying, "I saw you do it." Both the past-poster and the one I was about to pay took off at a fast pace for the door. The third one in the crew [a rounder], the one who'd distracted me by coming down late on the first third [the first twelve numbers] was long since gone. I realized I'd been past-posted. I hesitated to call the floorman over to tell him what happened, as I was the one responsible for protecting the game, but I did anyhow.

The shift boss went up to the eye in the sky and watched the video of the game. He told me later that it was the smoothest past-post he'd ever seen, and it was no wonder they'd gotten by with it. I was relieved to hear that, since according to the rules I could be punished. That's when he told me the past-posters were so good that I was going to get one week's suspension instead of getting fired. The suspension cost me about nine hundred dollars. When I came back to work, I dealt blackjack for the next four months, my real punishment for not catching the past-poster.

It makes you wonder, though, how many past-posters have put one down on you. I don't know. There may be teams out working the games that are better than the Middle Easterners, and they just haven't gotten caught. It's a thought.

1971

I was working relief dealer on a six-deck shoe, twenty minutes each at three different games. I'd just come on this particular game. Somehow, I got a strange feeling as soon as I did. You know the kind of feeling you get when your zipper's unzipped, and everyone else knows but you. The customers, well, three of them, reduced their bets as soon as I buried a card. One of them was watching my hand as I delivered the first card. It wasn't like he was looking to see what the card was, but studying how I moved the card from my left hand to my right and slid it to the appropriate player. I didn't hesitate, went on to the next card, and the next, on down the line. When each player was holding two cards, I started around the layout, hitting the players' hands when one or the other called for a hit.

The same player watched this action even more intently. Shortly after I'd dealt out two hands, one of the two bigger bettors on the game colored up for higher-denomination chips and left. Not long after that the guy watching me so closely got up from his seat. I knew something was wrong, and I called the nearest boss over. He called the eye in the sky.

Soon the boss returned, along with a shift boss. They talked a couple of minutes, then the floorman came over to my game with six fresh decks in hand. He tells me they're going to change the cards. This is pretty unusual. As one took cards from the discard rack, the other took the cards out of the shoe. They were in a hurry. I knew something was up. I hadn't even finished checking the first deck when the regular dealer assigned to the game returned from his break; I told him to finish checking the new deck and moved off to relieve the next game in the cycle.

Halfway through the shift, I was pulled up to the security office. The shift boss was there and so were some gaming agents or private detectives, the kind who look for cheaters. They wanted to know why I got suspicious. I couldn't explain exactly, just had a feeling. They asked if I could recognize the men who'd left. I said I could recognize the one who seemed to be studying me but probably not the others. I asked what it was about.

The boss laid four of the cards down before me and asked if I could see anything unusual. I had to look closely and didn't for the longest time, until he angled the side to the overhead light at approximately the same angle it would come out of the shoe. There on the edge, where the card would come out of the window, was a small dull mark.

"Sandpaper," the shift boss said.

He explained how someone had glued a speck of sandpaper to his finger and had used it to mark all the aces, face cards, and nines in the deck. Apparently they'd worked as a team, one signaling the other to hit, to stand, and so on. When I came on the game I kept the window covered with my left hand. The boss figured I spooked the cheaters.

Maybe. They'd sure spooked me. I was the hero for the night. The other dealer was fired. I felt sorry for him. I can see how it can happen. Go to sleep for twenty minutes on the game—bam, you're had.

1970s

I had this friend I dealt with downtown. This is back in the seventies. We were allowed to play slots on our breaks, and sometimes Dan and I would. I'd be playing the nickel slots, you know, a buck or so, and he'd be cranking on a dollar progressive, shoving in three bucks at a time. I didn't think much of it at first because he was dealing a little dope on the side, but then, too, I knew he was a pretty heavy user himself. Anyhow, I had a live-and-let-live view of the world, so I never said a thing.

One day I was on a game in the door. At the place I worked then, everyone pretty much knew it was cool to smoke dope or snort a line, and no one would say anything. In fact, a couple of security guards had caught some dealers doing a line and had called the cops. Metro booked the dealers. The guards were all gung-ho about busting the dealers, but when the general manager got wind of the arrest, he fired the two guards, and the dealers came back to work like nothing had happened. Anyhow, that day I had a couple of joints in my pocket that I was saving for my break. I was going to share one with my buddy Dan, who was on the next craps game dealing to some woman who's betting hundred-dollar chips.

I was on a twenty-five-cent game. It was a come-on game near the door, a low-limit table that brought players in. It was kind of boring, the same fleas gathered around the layout, except for a couple of guys on my end, pretty nicely dressed, you know, suits and ties, who seemed about half interested in what they were doing. They kept making late bets, you know, past-posting me, but it was obvious they weren't doing it because they knew how. They just weren't paying attention. Finally, I told them not to past-post me, that once the dice were in the air not to bet. They didn't try anymore.

Anyhow, my relief comes and taps me out. I clear my hands and make for the dealers' room. Our break room was down a narrow flight of stairs. I hurry to catch up with Dan. I'm just about to grab his shoulder and tell him that I have a number in my pocket when someone shoves me aside and grabs him. Then another guy jumps in. They push him away, turn him around, and put him in handcuffs. I'm beside myself. I think they have got the wrong guy, that they're after me and the joints I've got in my pocket. I figure I got lucky. I make it to the break room and toss the joints in the trash.

I didn't see Dan come down, so I had mixed feelings. I'd made it free and clear, but it was too bad for him. At the end of my break, I head up to the pit. Along the way I hear Dan was taken out. The cops were from the Gaming Control Board. They'd watched him for the whole hour that he'd dealt to the woman. I found out he was a chipmunk, that he'd come off the game with eight one-hundred-dollar chips in his mouth.

1976

I knew better than to get involved, but I did. It was the midseventies, and I was dealing at the Jolly Trolley at Sahara and the Strip. We were all young and a little crazy. You know, drugs and drinking and everyone was screwing everyone else. I'd been working at the Castaways for a few months before that. Got fired for no reason, except that was kind of the policy there if someone didn't like you. They fired you right before your vacation time was earned. Anyhow, I auditioned at a few spots but couldn't get a break. In those days everyone knew someone in other joints. One phone call, one bad word, you're out. So I took the job at the Trolley.

It was kind of interesting, a combination topless dance joint and small casino. Gambling and sex. Every once in a while some tourist from Des Moines or wherever would stumble in with his wife on his arm and a camera dangling from his neck. He'd take a minute to adjust to the light, then bam! Him and the wife would see the bare breasts, have a coronary, and fly out the door. I used to get a kick out of that. What we pretty much accepted as normal was way out there for others. Looking back, I can see how I got caught up in everything, which is no excuse. I could have turned the deal down.

This guy—I'll call him "Art"—used to hang out in the joint. He drank a bit and gambled and was involved with one of the dancers. Let's call her "Mandy." One night at the close of shift Mandy's girlfriend Lu came over to my game and asked me to buy her a drink. She was hot. I'd had my eye on her for a long time. I looked her up and down and thought, what the hell, I'd walk through a burning desert to make her. By eight-fifteen I'm having my second beer, and Lu's hanging on my arm like we've been an item for months. She asks me to take her home. I was ready. We peeled out of there like the roof on the joint was about to collapse.

A week later I was still taking Lu home every night after work and smiling the whole way. One night she told me that Art wanted to meet me. We were supposed to catch up with him and Mandy at the Golden Steer, which was about two hundred yards right up the street on Sahara. We walked over there, Lu hooked to my arm like she always was, me feeling like my bank account had accidentally been credited with ten thousand cash. Art and Mandy had gotten a booth near the back. Lu introduced us. I said I knew him from dealing to him. He was a stiff, but I didn't mention this. He asked what we were drinking. Lu wanted champagne. Art didn't hesitate. We had a bottle of champagne on the table the rest of the night. When the meal was over, Art took all of us out to see a lounge act at the Sahara and then over to the Slipper to catch *Boylesque*. We smoked a joint along the way. By the time we got to the Slipper, we were feeling pretty okay with the world. I remember the parking valet getting in the car and smiling at us as if to say he knew the smell of good dope. Art crossed his lips with an index finger and gave him a ten. The guy said something like, "Anything you say, Bud."

After that Lu and I were an item, and the four of us got together a couple of nights a week. Art never spoke to me when he came into the casino, said it was better to keep a distance there. He didn't come in all that often anyhow. One night about a month after I started dating Lu, she told me Art wanted me to come over to his townhouse. He lived on the Las Vegas Country Club right off Karen Street. It was an upscale place, two bedrooms with Danish furniture and a gray carpet. He opened the door and welcomed us like we were VIPs. Mandy was sitting on the couch in bikini briefs and nothing else, watching the television. She didn't even look up. Lu patted my arm and went over to the couch to watch with Mandy. Art told me to follow him upstairs, said he had something to run by me in private.

On the way upstairs he paused on the landing and said, "I want to make it clear that this is between us."

I nodded, but I was getting a queer feeling in my stomach. He pointed out the master bedroom, which had a circular bed, and told me that was the "playroom." He opened the door to the second bedroom and stepped aside.

"The office," he said.

The office was a room with two blackjack tables and two walls and the ceiling mirrored. I said it was impressive. He asked me how I'd like to make a lot of money. My stomach kind of went upside down. I asked how.

"You know what a cooler is?"

I'd heard the term before, knew it had something to do with cheating. I nodded.

"Think you got the balls to take one?"

I knew full well that getting caught cheating was a guaranteed way to get blackballed from casinos. I knew it was a prison sentence. I said I didn't know if I had guts enough to do it. He told me to sit down at the nearest table. He took a deck and dealt me a blackjack hand. I won. Then another and another, until the deck was almost gone. I never lost a hand.

"A piece of cake," he said and explained how all we had to do was practice the moves to get the old deck out and the cooler in on a game, said he'd have the table stacked with two players, playing all the spaces. They'd be in and out in fifteen minutes, and I'd be richer by five grand. We'd do it three, maybe four times a year, and he knew people at Caesars and the Trop who could get me a better job, people who'd be interested in doing a little business.

Twenty grand would more than double my yearly income, but that wasn't the reason I said yes. I used a convoluted pattern of reasoning to look at Art's proposition. The casinos didn't give a damn about me. Wasn't I fired from the Castaways so they wouldn't have to give me a paid vacation? Didn't casinos take advantage of people? What was more boring than being a dealer? I wanted to escape the mundane repetition, wanted to be like Art, toss money around and own a classy townhouse. I liked having an exotic dancer hold on to my arm. It was ego.

Before the night was over I said I would. It didn't occur as a contradiction to me that if Art had connections at Caesars and the Trop, why would he want to cheat the Jolly Trolley? I saw Lu on my arm, money to buy drugs, money to party on, a new car. I saw everything but what I should have seen.

We practiced every night for a week, two, three hours, using a double deck. I didn't get to meet the players. It was Art's way of protecting things. I had good hands. From the get-go I'd been a good clerk. This was just one more move. I passed off the old deck as I set it out to be cut. He gave me the cooler with a cut card already in it. We practiced the timing over and over, watching ourselves in the mirrors. Sometimes Mandy was in the room and would work with us, blocking or rounding as the moves were called, the idea being to distract anyone who might be watching the game. And she had plenty to work with in the distraction department.

On the last night Art brought up a bottle of champagne for us, and Mandy and Lu had sex with each other on one of the tables. I admit this bothered me a lot, but I was in now, and it was part of the scene. Art asked me if I wanted to go with the two ladies myself. We lit up a joint. Art took a hit or two, told me to have a good time, then excused himself. When I came downstairs, he was sitting in front of the television staring at the screen, but the sound was off.

"Don't freeze," he said. "That's the only thing. Don't freeze."

Three nights later Art showed up at my game. A man and a woman had been playing for about a half-hour and were down about three hundred dollars and starting to chase after their losses. Art asked if it was windy outside, which was the signal that the exchange would go down after the next shuffle. Mandy was standing next to him with a drink in her hand. I realized that the couple on the game were the ones set up to play off the cooler and began the shuffle. Saying I was nervous would be like saying a man facing execution is curious about his future. The floorman was watching. Don't freeze, I told myself, but I had a serious moment of panic as I finished the shuffle, wondering how we were going to get around him.

The feeling was worse than anything I'd imagined but at the same time exhilarating. It was as if every eye in the place was looking at me, hundreds of them, through a magnifying glass. I had two choices—walk away or do it. I took a deep breath and hoped my hand wouldn't shake too noticeably when I offered the deck for Art to cut. Just before I extended the deck to Art, Mandy set her drink on the edge of the table and spilled it on the man who was playing.

"I'm so sorry," she said, her eyes all wide and innocent.

The player stepped back and held his hands out, flicking scotch and soda off his fingertips, looking irritated, as if he weren't part of the scam. His trousers were also wet. Mandy apologized again.

Quick wit won the moment. When the floorman bent down to get a table towel from under my table, I offered the deck to Art and he swept it from my left hand and popped the cooler in my right so fast that I didn't see it. I was adjusting the deck to my palm to deal when the floorman stood up and passed the towel to the player. The pass went down as smooth as a quail's breast, and we would have gotten by with it if not for a change girl who thought she saw something and reported it to the shift boss. By then Art and Mandy were gone. He'd played a token hand, lost, and left. The man, finished with dabbing the drink off his trousers, stepped up to the game steady and cool as a river rock and bet the table limit on three hands. The woman and he played and were up eight grand or so when security came up to the table, and the boss yanked the deck out of my hand.

They put us in handcuffs and called the cops.

I was the only one convicted. The cops and the Gaming Commission wanted me to testify against the others, but I refused the deals. By then I figured I'd messed up on my own. I wasn't going to blame Art or Mandy or Lu. I copped a plea and got off fairly light, a year in the county jail, done in seven months, and five years' probation. But I was out of the casinos as far as dealing went. Twenty-four, an ex-felon with no other work skills, my work card pulled, I got a job teaching black-jack in a dealing school. Eleven years later I got everything expunged, but you can't expunge certain records. My mugshots were in a black book circulated in casinos.

I never dealt another hand, but in time I worked my way back into the business. Now I park my butt in a chair and watch games from the eye in the sky, a hundred forty-five a shift and a free meal. What else can thieves do in this business but catch thieves? I work with a couple of others who scammed joints in the past. One of them said that at one time everyone in the business had a past. Now it's all clean. At least that's the image. What's ironic is that the people who hire for casinos just assume because I'm in Griffin Detective Agency's cheater book that I was good at stealing and knew something. "Knowledgeable" is how they refer to someone like me. How could they know I only stole once and got caught the first time? I'd say ignorant is the opposite of knowledgeable, and that's as profound as I'm going to get.

1993

They treat hustling like it's cheating, you know, even the soft hustle if the dice are rolling bad for the house. Let's face it, if you don't go out for a dime, you ain't gonna make shit. A lotta joints are splitting tokes between craps and twenty-one, which has made craps dealers lazy and a bit snarly with customers. I mean, if your living depends on being nice to someone, then that's what you are. If, on the other hand, you've got a bunch of blackjack dealers whoring for tokes, why risk going out with your palm open? For what, to be called a thief and get fired?

I was on two crews at two different joints where we were fired for hustling. What's hypocritical is that the house wants us to go out and hustle proposition bets 'cause they're strong for the joint. I know that some craps crews strong-arm the players, and players bitch. I mean, I've worked on crews where we'd tell a player to put a fiver down next to his line bet and then take the odds, both for us. But we're also helping the guy by telling him the best way to win, and we're rootin' for him, too, which makes him feel damn good. When was the last time you saw a casino manager standing beside a craps game that was out of hand and cheering for the players? If you ask me, the house is cheating the players by hustling proposition bets. That's how I see it. If I'm cheating, then what the hell would you call what the house does?

1960s

When I first went to work for the Sands, it was flatter than an aircraft carrier deck. That was in the Rat Pack days, when the Sands was the queen of the Strip. The big players came to the Sands to maybe catch a glimpse of Sinatra or Dean Martin, who sometimes played in the casino. A high roller didn't have a prayer. Every shift had a couple of mechanics, and the craps crews would pay off a winning roll, and every player at the table ended up losing on the roll. Inside the joint they were referred to as "firemen." They'd come onto a game to put out the fire. It was a game to them, an insider kind of thing where they get the joke, but no one else does. Those guys were treated real special, like the goose that laid the golden egg, which they were. Of course, we were all treated damn good then, not like now, where you're just another cow in the herd.

There was this one kid who'd learned the business from his dad and uncle. He was, I think, from Montana. He'd do things with a deck that were amazing and never a hint that anything was up. He showed me one time how he could switch his hole card and deal seconds. I never saw a thing that looked abnormal in his delivery. Of course, the bosses were working for people who expected the joint to win, no matter, and there was skimming going on, and money going to the Mob.

I was at the Sands a couple of years when it was still flat. Then one day we went to dealing out of shoes. I heard that the Gaming Control Board told the top bosses they better start dealing out of shoes or else the doors would be shut. But the craps crews were still hitting the players pretty good. All that ended when Howard Hughes bought the Sands. A lot of things changed in this town when Hughes arrived. I wonder what happened to those mechanics? Probably ended up bosses somewhere else. I'll take the old days to what I got now, flat stores, Mob, and all. But that kind of cheating could have ruined the state if it'd gone on and on. I know it. It was all a game back then.

1983

We worked the graveyard crew in craps, the same seven guys, plus the occasional fill-in from someone in blackjack. One game was all we kept open after four o'clock. It was usually real slow, so we'd talk to one another, spread the bull. The fella that sat box with us mostly was this big old guy from Arkansas. He'd been a dealer in the old days in Hot Springs. That was as a young man. Now he was about sixty. We liked him, but his personality kind of changed whenever the dice went bad for the house. You know, a sweater. He acted like it was his own money. He'd grumble and growl at us. Still, we'd let him in on the conversations and pretend he didn't have that annoying habit of worrying about the house's money.

Like I said, it was slow on graveyard some of the time. This old guy would come into the pit with a mug of coffee and set it on the podium right behind us. Whenever the game went dead, he'd stand up and stretch, then grab a drink out of the mug. We gave this no never mind. Then one morning, the shift boss, security, and the eye in the sky marched into the pit with some cops. It was like a Gestapo raid. First thing they do is grab the mug of coffee. One of them, can't remember who, pours the coffee slowly into the wastebasket. Don't you know there were two green checks in there. This old box man goes pale. He tried to talk, but all the southern was knocked out of his accent. They handcuffed him, and off he went. They pulled a dealer out of the twenty-one pit and had him sit box.

It gave us something new to talk about for a few days whenever the game went dead. We talked about that guy and how he sweated the money like it was his own. Guess he figured taking a little bit was okay since he'd spent so much time worrying about it. Tell you the truth, I've forgotten his name. That's how it is. You're worth a few days' talk and not much else.

1972

Ash Resnick was an exec at Caesars. His claim to fame was having played with the old Boston Celtics. He was a kind of brash guy, a bit like Bobby Knight who coached Indiana, and was supposed to be connected. Who knows? I don't, but he pretty much ran the joint. That much I know.

One week he had some housemen come in to watch some of the blackjack dealers who were suspected of being involved in a scam. An ex-boxer who was dealing blackjack and drugs had snitched them off. The guys were passing off to agents. I'm not sure how exactly—over-paying or just paying on every hand, even losers. Something like that. Ash's housemen busted one of the dealers when the guy left the game and met a girl who'd been playing on his game. The agent had followed the girl to the cage, where she'd cashed out a few hundred. This dealer took the money from her in the hallway by the shopping promenade. That's how bold these guys were. I knew they were dealing coke and speed and pretty over the line.

Ash fired them. In those days no one in the casino business wanted to prosecute. Ash, being the cocky guy he was, figured it was over. A few nights later he was driving home east on Flamingo Road. This was when it was two lanes before all the development, and there were patches of desert on both sides. This car had been following him. Near Eastern Avenue it pulled around him, and someone wearing a Halloween mask started shooting. As the first of the rounds smashed his window, Ash Resnick ducked below the steering wheel and took his Cadillac straight out into the desert. The bullets barely missed their mark. A few days later he got lucky again. This time someone had poured a couple of gallons of acid into his swimming pool at home. Of course, the cops investigated both incidents and had some strong suspects, but no leads and no evidence. Ash moved into Caesars Palace for a couple of weeks, supposedly to have his house remodeled. Rumor had it that he was working out a deal to get the heat off. Seems two of the dealers involved were connected to the Mob through their fathers. In time Ash returned to his home. He was never exactly what you could call humble after that, but he was changed. Watchful.

1971

When I was at the Stardust, we had this dealer who cut tokes until one shift he was caught stuffing ten extra envelopes. That was ten envelopes for dealers who simply didn't exist. We weren't making even fifty a shift most days. Anyhow, this guy got nailed and fired. It happens, money being so readily available and human nature being what it is. He was gone. We were glad. I didn't think a thing of it.

A few nights go by, and I walk into Circus Circus at the end of my shift. Of course, that's about the end of their shift as well. What do I see but this same guy who'd gotten fired at the Stardust for stealing dealers' tokes. He's carrying a box full of chips—the dealers' toke box. My jaw dropped. Imagine!

1994

I'd been cutting tokes at the end of the shift for more than a year. We used her—I'll call her "Emmy" because she deserves one for her performance—to help out because it was hard to get volunteers. At the end of the shift most everybody wanted to head home or straight to the bar. I don't know what exactly made me suspicious. Maybe it was the way Emmy always went for the twenty-five-dollar checks. We'd pick up the toke boxes, undo our work ties, and loosen our collars and pour the chips out on this metal-top table in the count room downstairs. Emmy plowed into the greens like God had sent her on a mission.

She and I were friends. You know, work friends. We'd get together sometimes in the break room and talk about our kids or our ex-husbands. Never much nice there. I liked her. That's what hurts. She just wasn't the one you'd figure, but she had habits. Booze and gambling. Gets to a lot of people in the business. But she was a mother. Being one myself, I just figure kids come first.

Anyhow, I spot her going to her waist with her hand like she's adjusting the shirt. When I saw it a second time, I got suspicious. Well, we had cameras in the count room. They weren't on us but on the people who did the count and worked the window. So, I figured I'd give her another shot before I acted. Next evening it's the same thing—mucking up greens, stacking them, adjusting her shirt at the waist. I don't say anything. What's the point?

I reported what I'd seen to the shift boss and pitboss. They put the camera on us for the next two days to gather evidence. I don't tell a soul, which is hard for me because, quite frankly, I like to gossip. It makes the job interesting. But this stuff about Emmy is locked inside my head. Besides, what if I was wrong? You just can't go around accusing people. Friday came and went, and security didn't confront her.

Next day at work she was her usual, just lovely this and just lovely that. We talked about the kids and the rotten husbands we were glad to be rid of. I didn't let on. I smiled and played it up better than Sarah Bernhardt. At the end of the shift, and it was a Saturday so my rear was dragging, and so was everyone else's, we go downstairs. I unhook my bow tie and dump the boxes. She sits down, and we start the small talk. Two other dealers are with us because Saturday is the biggest day of the week. I didn't say a thing to them, didn't want to alert them. About twenty minutes into the cut, the door opens, and a male and female security guard come in with the shift boss on their heels.

Emmy looks up, and it's written all over her face. Guilty. The rest of us look up, then look at her. They ask her to go with them. She wasn't arrested, she got fired. I wanted her arrested. They had the whole thing on tape, not one day but three. The joint won't prosecute and won't let the dealers prosecute. Hey, it's our money, not theirs. But that's how it is in the business. Dealers don't even have the right to file a criminal complaint because the house is afraid of publicity and wasting their time in court on something that's not their concern. Pretty sweet for the thieves, whose termination slips say "change of personnel" or "violation of house rules." It's pretty bogus.

Emmy got another job. We found out she'd been playing poker ma-chines pretty heavy. A few days after she was fired, Emmy called me at home and asked how I could do it, said she thought we were good friends. I told her that friends don't steal from friends and coworkers don't steal from coworkers. She said it was just once that she was des-perate. I figured she'd beat us dealers out of about fifteen grand mini-mum. That's not small change. She started crying. I hung up. How can you have sympathy in a situation like that?

The other truth is that if she'd been stealing from the house, they would have marched her through the casino in handcuffs and prose-cuted her. And some judge would have given her jail time. Judges in Nevada have no patience with thieves who steal from casinos. This happens in every joint I ever worked. All you can do is keep an eye out and don't trust anyone who's touching your money.

6

COPING

Many dealers take pride in their work, in the skills that it takes to keep a game moving along at a strong, steady pace. Years go into honing finger dexterity to the degree that hand and mind coordinate complex moves seemingly without willful effort. Dealers simply assume a kind of mistake-free competence in themselves. It's the job, and when one does make a mistake, she's as mystified by it as the customers who witness it. If laborers in other businesses worked as mistake-free as dealers, American industry would be without parallel. It is this extreme measure of competence that makes dealers feel unappreciated. They assume that management and customers alike should appreciate the skill a dealer demonstrates, hour in, hour out, day in, day out. But this doesn't happen. Nor is it realistic for dealers to expect any kind of praise. The occasional word from a boss when a dealer comes off a "monster" game goes as far as a big tip in making the dealer's day. "You dealt a clean game" is high praise and seldom heard.

Over the three decades from the sixties through the eighties several attempts were begun to organize dealers into unions. In every case the unions lost out, not always by vote. Casino management appealed vote after vote, fought organizing at every level—including initiating bills at the state legislature to make it unlawful for employees to sue based on false termination. In the late seventies, when Las Vegas was hit hard by inflation and recession, more than forty male dealers, most of them over forty, were fired at the Las Vegas Hilton. These men were replaced by younger dealers, mostly women. The men took their case to the Nevada Equal Rights Commission and eventually federal court, where they prevailed and were awarded money for damages that amounted on the average to $200,000 per man. The Hilton appealed the award, and the courts chipped away at the figures until years later the dealers ended up with about twelve cents on the dollar. Some of the dealers lost homes and families. A few died before the case was settled. The message was clear: Don't go up against casinos in Nevada. They have the "deep pockets and all the connections." The other part of the message is that dealers are too plentiful to be of value, no matter how long they've worked for a company.

One of the problems is that worker turnover in the gaming business is higher than in many other trades. Additionally, dealers don't form communities outside of work. Exhausted and looking for sanctuary at the end of a shift, they go to the confines of their homes or someplace for a quiet drink. A few go out and gamble, which seems as strange as a homemaker going to her neighbor's house to clean it. In short, dealers don't organize themselves. The huge influx of women and immigrant Asians into the casino business has further retarded any union movements. There has to be a strong sense of dissatisfaction for laborers to organize, and women, now earning considerably more than they're used to, haven't yet reached the level of dissatisfaction necessary to organize. The same reasoning can be applied to immigrant Asians. Perhaps that's why the union movement died in the nineties—that along with a period of unprecedented growth and prosperity. The issue of organizing dealers is critical, a labor activity that casinos continue to resist, one in which the dealers have demonstrated time after time that they are unwilling to cooperate and sacrifice long enough to establish a union. Who knows, this kind of complacency may change, but as of the turn of the century there was no groundswell to organize dealers.

In defense of the casino industry, it's only fair to mention that many resorts have taken it upon themselves to improve conditions for dealers. Several have set up appeal processes to deal with wrongful terminations or sexual harassment or complaints against supervisors. Some have initiated reward programs for outstanding employees, but these usually pertain directly to customer service and not to the other skills that dealers must employ, such as speed and accuracy. Other casinos have experimented with the "team" approach and solicit input from dealers on decisions critical to them. Benefits have improved, including the introduction of retirement programs in many casinos during the eighties.

Despite all the other improvements, wages have not increased to any degree. In the early sixties, bartenders and dealers made the same approximate wage and tips above and beyond that. By the nineties this figure had changed radically. Bartenders now make, on the average, three times per shift what dealers make. Figures of $39 per day versus $148 per day are common. Depending on what station the bartender works, his or her tips may exceed those of a dealer. Casinos won't bend on the issue of wages, citing tips as the actual compensation for work. Yet in some ways management determines how much dealers make in tips. Some casinos have limited the credit of high rollers who they think tip too much. Some have gone so far as to cut off a player's credit for "over tipping." And every casino has a maximum bet allowed for the dealers.

One of the worst parts of the system that dealers work under is favoritism. Most commonly called "juice," this system is so entrenched in the casino industry that promotions and jobs, especially at desirable joints, are determined by who knows whom. Those who don't have juice try to get juice. Those who have it use it like armor or, in some cases, weaponry. A pretty woman has no trouble getting juice, but if she doesn't do something for her juice, she won't last long. A man can get juice in a variety of ways, some of which include playing golf with the boss, putting a patio in the boss's backyard, giving a boss tickets to a college basketball game. The list goes on and on, as do the inequities. If the world is unfair, casinos are even more unfair.

Dealers have pretty much stuck to the standard actions in dealing with real and perceived injustices: They joke or bitch. What other choices do they have? It's the nature of the business. So much of what goes on inside a casino is esoteric that outsiders can't fully appreciate what's at stake. A lot of what's at stake is the dealer's humanity, his or her dignity. Dealers define themselves by how they perform and how much they are compensated. The compensation is not always enough, but the performance must always be sufficient. Dealers, reconciled to accepting what comes their way, compensate for life's imbalances by telling stories, by gambling themselves, by drinking, going home to the kids, playing basketball or tennis, growing flowers, hiking, taking trips. In short, they find lives outside the casino, and those who don't are usually pretty miserable.

1987

I was recruited into the Nevada Casino Dealers' Association in 1987 ostensibly to help write and edit copy. I even resisted joining but was worn down by the core of dealers who formed it. I was given a title, which meant nothing. I wanted to do my part. At the time, the casino industry and other businesses were engaged in lobbying for legislation to prevent employees from suing for unwarranted terminations. Having gone through one such mass layoff, I felt strongly about the issue. It's a citizen's right to sue, and if the courts are taken away from the little guy and handed over to the rich special interests, what recourse does the little guy have?

At any rate, I attended the occasional meeting, added a suggestion or two here and there, but wasn't too deeply involved. In fact, I usually took the moderate stance, arguing that persuasion goes a lot further than confrontation. The association was no different than any other political action committee or organization of professionals. The platform was political and designed to look out for the welfare of dealers. It was never intended as a union. It's possible that some of the personnel rules favorable to dealers and other employees were instituted because the association was active and vocal. The president, Tony Badillo, wrote letters and press releases to publicize injustices in casino policies. Association members picketed the state legislature on one issue. I once went on a late night show and discussed the objectives of the association. All in all, it was nominally effective as an organization and hardly the type that threatened the casinos.

In the early nineties I left Las Vegas for about a year. I returned for a short visit over Christmas and looked up some dealers I'd worked with at the Las Vegas Hilton. We were sitting around drinking and playing Pictionary when one of the women told me she'd seen my mugshot on a podium at the Las Vegas Hilton. All dealers have mugshots taken for their work permits, and this was a recent one, according to the woman. A second dealer, a man, confirmed the story. Others, too, had seen it and commented.

One of the bosses had explained to them that my photo along with Tony Badillo's and a couple of others' were circulated to several casinos. I later uncovered information that suggested that the Griffin Detective Agency was behind the distribution of the mugs and that the agency had obtained the names of the officers from the articles of incorporation filed with the state of Nevada. My name was listed as a titled officer of the association. I was appalled, even tempted to contact an attorney, after I found out I was being treated as a common criminal, someone the casinos should stop and issue a trespass warning to. For what? Political activities. Casinos, having privileged legal status, can bar anyone from working or even entering a casino on threat of arrest.

I understood fully what circulating the mugshots meant. If word got out, I would be blackballed from the industry, or at least that part of the industry served by Griffin Investigations. I wasn't a thief. My work record had been impeccable. I'd worked in the industry for more than a dozen years at five different casinos. That, in short, is why the dealers need an association to protect them. I'm no longer in the casino business, nor do I belong to the Nevada Casino Dealers' Association, but every time I go into a casino, for whatever purpose, I wonder if someone will see me and associate my face with a mugshot, if I will be escorted to the door by security and asked to leave or perhaps arrested. If it ever happens, there will be a lawsuit. As far as I know, no other industry bar members of political action groups, if those groups are not disturbing the peace, from free access to public spaces.

I look back on my days in the casinos, on the positive aspects and the negative ones, and I can say that I don't regret having worked in the casinos. At times it was drudgery. At times it was fun. I had some laughs, and I'm not bitter. But I'm leery of any institution that tries to suppress human rights. Unfortunately, eliminating such obvious injustices won't occur in the legislature or the governor's office. It'll take the courts to rein in the power of the casino industry in Nevada.

1983

There was this dealer, Jake. I won't mention his last name as he's still in the business, I think. His father-in-law was a big executive at another joint, a shift boss or casino manager, I think. Anyhow, Jake was a big, pushy kind of guy in his late thirties, a rough-talking type, who dropped his father-in-law's name whenever he could. He wasn't real well liked. I worked graveyard with him. Things were usually pretty slow after five in the morning until about nine or ten, so we got lots of breaks. We'd go upstairs to the dealers' room and play pitch or tonk, one- and two-dollar hands.

Over a period of time Jake started having trouble with a couple of bosses. He was the kind who hated to be told anything. You know the kind, always right. Well, Jake took offense at being corrected, but he had game habits that violated procedure—the way he held chips in his deck hand and would cut out blackjack payoffs outside the circle or not cut into checks when he was paying off. One of the bosses on the shift was a guy named Gary. He was pretty rigid, more rigid than some sergeants I'd encountered in the army. He went by the book and had corrected Jake's procedure a few times. The more he was corrected, the more Jake went out of his way to ignore whatever he was told.

For about three weeks Jake kept claiming he'd had enough. He said more than once he was going to sucker punch Gary or the other boss. I can't remember the other floorman's name, but he was a serious black belt in some martial art, not someone to mess with. We told Jake that if he hit the other guy, he better kill him or run. Jake said we were full of it. Well, lucky for Jake that the night he decided to take his swing, Gary was on duty, and the other floorman wasn't.

Sure enough, Jake set it up. Gary was behind him when Jake gave a player a hit card using his deck hand. Gary said he wanted to see Jake when he came off the game. I didn't see the punch because I was down the pit dealing, but I heard it and heard Gary hit the floor. As I said, Jake was a big man, well over two hundred pounds, while Gary probably weighed in at one-thirty. It sounded bad. Jake hit him and walked out of the pit, went to the time office, and checked out. No one tried to stop him. Security didn't arrest him. Gary lay on his back, completely unconscious for four or five minutes. He was hurt real bad. He went to the hospital and was off for a while. As I recall, he wore a neck brace when he came back.

Jake called in the next day and asked if he was on the schedule to work. The guy was in a world of his own. What's strange is that he skated on what he did. I heard that his father-in-law got him a job somewhere else. Someone in the know said that management talked Gary out of filing a complaint with the authorities because it could cause bad publicity. Someone else said it was because Jake's father-in-law had heavy juice. Either way, that's the business.

When Gary came back to work, nothing changed. He was as hard nosed as ever. Some of us who'd heard the threats Jake had made were asked why we didn't report them to management. Most of us just hadn't taken him seriously. A couple said they were hoping that Jake would hit the karate guy and get his ass kicked. Jake was a bit of a bully, so that made sense. A couple of other dealers said they wanted Jake to hit Gary. Mostly we didn't say anything because no one wanted to be a snitch or get involved in someone else's business. It tells you something about people. The business puts a lot of pressure on people, a lot of stress. Maybe that's what it is. Some dealers just lose perspective. It's a little sick, for sure. I know one thing—Gary had some serious job security after that punch he took. I told him he should sue the joint.

1975

This happened on my crew at the Golden Nugget. This player spilled a beer. He'd been drinking quite a bit. Anyhow, the guy on third base got a table towel and tossed it to the player and asked him to wipe it up. The player mopped up some of the beer and instead of handing the towel back, threw it in the dealer's face. The dealer clapped out, walked around the table, and started punching the player out. He didn't let up even as security guards dragged him off. We all have a breaking point; this one was his.

1970s

I was working at the Stardust when this happened. We had this young dealer, a break-in, but not too bad. He looked like a kid. Ends up he was. Someone found out he was the sheriff's kid. Imagine. This kid had a sheriff's card that said he was legal age and a job making about forty grand a year, and he was only nineteen. Hell, he wasn't legally allowed in the joint, much less to work behind a blackjack layout. He didn't get arrested or anything, but the Gaming Control Board put some heat on the Stardust, and the newspapers put some heat on the sheriff. I think the sheriff was quoted in the paper as saying it was a mistake. A what? If it had been your kid or mine, that child would have gone to jail. A mistake! I call it an intentional.

1970s

The Showboat's policy was for us to be friendly and to greet players when they sat down at our games. Most of us were pretty good about it. Once in a while someone would forget to tell a player hello, and that dealer would get counseled. No matter how hard you try, some people can't be satisfied. That's the hard part, because management doesn't take into consideration all the variables that go into dealing with the public day in and day out. Sometimes it just gets to a guy.

Take Pete, for example. I worked with him at the 'Boat. He was an okay guy and not bad with the customers, a big Greek man with a thick accent. One night this customer comes up to Pete's game. Pete says whatever he said to greet the player, who took exception to the way Pete said it. So the player goes to the pitboss and pitches a grievance about how he was greeted, then the player goes back to the game and tells Pete what he did. When Pete comes off the game, a boss reams him out. Pete doesn't say anything. He's lost a few minutes of his break and taken a little grief, but that's that.

Pete walked out of the pit, and as he did, the player said something. Pete walked out muttering, started for the break room, thought better of it, then walked over and flicked the player in the back of the head with a middle finger. He didn't even slow down after that, just went to the time office and punched out. Guess you could say he hit his breaking point. I don't know what happened to him after that. The player, I think, threatened to sue. Where that went, I have no idea.

UNDATED

What amazes me most is that no one has ever come into a casino pit and just started blasting. All the kooks out there everywhere and some pretty uptight casino workers, yet so far no one's taken a pit out. I've been in the business a lot of years and have witnessed some pretty disgruntled players and employees, and years ago the casinos laid people off like it was a necessary transfusion or something. I mean, there's a lot of crap you have to put up with. Lucky is what I'd say we are. Hell, look at what happens at the post office and in restaurants, places like that. It'll happen, though. Wait and see. Too many kooks out there. Way too many.

UNDATED

I really liked dealing with a hand deck. I worked on my pitch, practicing it hour after hour as I watched television. There's something about being so good at something that your fellow workers watch you do it. I could have three, sometimes four, cards in the air at the same time. And I was fast and accurate. When you have a skill like that, it draws people to the game, especially if there's any action.

The best I ever felt about myself when I was dealing was when I had to work a heavy game, and I'd come off it, and the floorman or pitboss would say something as small as "You dealt a clean game." That's praise to a real clerk. We don't want to hear we're great or the best or any of that stuff. A clean game. That says everything. But it never meant a thing as far as privilege goes. If you don't know someone, you may as well know nothing.

1990s

Every so often they clock us for a GPA, a game pace average. You have to sign the sheet. The way they do it is to count the number of hands you get out in fifteen minutes and multiply that by four. I was never under 250. I don't know how that stacked up, but the bosses always said I could do better. I figured it out one day, and if I won an average of a dollar a hand that's two grand a day I make for the joint. They pay me thirty-nine bucks a day, and the players tip me, according to the average I pick up in my envelopes, about one hundred and twenty a day. That makes me worth, at a dollar a hand, $1,861 per day. If I had someone making me that kind of money, I'd just kiss his ass and say "thank you."

1995

It was like two o'clock in the afternoon, and my relief was late as usual, this time about three or four minutes. I was about to call the floorman over and have him page the jerk when I saw my relief hurrying down the escalator, taking two steps at a time. He almost fell stepping onto the casino floor. When he got to the pit, he hurried down to tap me out.

"Sorry," he said, "I got tied up giving a customer directions. I'll make it up to you next break."

I looked over my shoulder. He's standing off to the side. I have to look up to see his face, and when I do, I notice the white powder on his nostrils.

"Did you have to put your spoon up to give directions?"

"What?"

I spread my deck and stepped back. "You may want to wipe the coke off your nose," I whispered.

He ran his sleeve across his nose and stepped up to the game. I don't know if any of the players noticed anything or overheard us, but my relief was sure nervous. He came down early to take me off the game the next two breaks. I never mentioned what happened. I'm a woman, but I don't believe in snitching. Some dealers would have gone to a boss. Not me, not even to make a jerk pay his dues.

1980s

This guy got juiced in at Caesars. His uncle was one of the top executives, which is a sugar-coated title for a boss who's got hidden interests. Jewish Mob. Anyhow, this kid had a serious Quaalude habit, not one or two but four during a shift. It wasn't like we weren't all dropping 'ludes in those days, but he ate them like corn chips.

One night this guy is almost zombied out. You could see him swaying behind the game. The bosses don't pay any attention because he's so hooked up. Who lands on his game but the headliner that week, whose name I won't say on the record, but who's a very popular singer. The entertainer is betting greens on two hands, no more than a hundred bucks a hand. It's good for the joint to have an entertainer play at the games. Gives the high rollers someone to rub elbows with. Our man was so stoned he probably didn't know who he was dealing to.

The entertainer had twenty-five bet on his second hand, and the dealer pointed to it and in so doing essentially asked if he wanted a hit. The entertainer had a seventeen and signaled "no" with a sweep of his hand. The dealer hit the hand anyhow. With a three! He pointed to the hand again. And again, the entertainer signaled "no." The dealer hit him again, this time with a face card. Then hit again. The entertainer, who's a very nice guy, didn't say a word. The cards kept coming out of the shoe and ending up on the entertainer's hand. Finally, the dealer couldn't place another card down because he was no longer standing. He simply passed out.

When the boss turned around, he saw a dealer lying on the floor and the entertainer staring at the hand in front of him, which had to be a world's record for blackjack, since it totaled up to fifty-four. The boss asked the entertainer why he hadn't said something, to which the entertainer said that he didn't want to get the dealer in trouble.

The dealer was off for a couple of days, then came back. That's how it was. Eventually he got himself fired. You can get by with it for only so long before your juice can't take the heat himself.

1980

There was this craps dealer on our shift who could get you anything. He called himself the "Candy Man." One year Amy threw a Christmas party at her house. She had a nice two-story home somewhere off Desert Inn and Rainbow. All I remember about her was that she was small and friendly. She didn't do drugs or cause anyone any problems. She was nice, I guess you'd say.

Anyhow, the party takes place at her house a couple of days before Christmas. It was an open-house party, bring your own bottle. She provided snacks, bread and cookies, etc. She had a rumpus room marked off for dancing, and music came from her stereo and was piped throughout the house. People were talking, mostly shop, which is why I hate parties like that. Some people are drinking and smoking cigarettes. Now and then a couple of people drifted outside to light up a joint. They tried to be inconspicuous. It was the polite thing to do because they were guests. It's a pretty calm party, everyone behaving and having a good time.

About one o'clock the Candy Man shows up. His crew has been let off early. He's wearing a Santa Claus outfit, red and white, with a gray wig and false beard, but there was no doubting who it was. An hour or so later the Candy Man and this guy he just met were having a conversation about doing a cocaine deal. Not long after that he left and was gone for about forty minutes. When he came back, he had a package and scales with him. He and the other guy sat down at Amy's dining room table and commenced to conduct business.

Mind you, we were a pretty tolerant group. Most of us had smoked a little weed during the night, and a couple of people had gone out to their cars to toot up, but this was a total breach of etiquette. I went over to the table and said it would be a good idea to take it elsewhere. The Candy Man made some off-the-cuff remark, like I was some kind of prudish hall monitor or something. I was ready to take his head off, but Amy asked me not to. She asked them both to leave. They finished the deal and left, no apology or anything, just a sarcastic "Ho, ho, merry Christmas" from the Candy Man as he shut the door.

What does it do for you, seeing Santa Claus do a cocaine deal on an innocent woman's maple dining set? It's pretty damned disillusioning is what it is. After that I kind of avoided parties and socializing with other dealers I worked with. It was much easier to see them at work.

1985?

The drugs are still out there. Oh, they test us randomly, and if someone's looking a little too high, they'll pull him off and take him to the clinic for a drug test. But it's not as blatant as it was in the old days, by which I mean the seventies and the eighties. There were some joints where people got jobs because they were dealers. The pun is intended.

I worked at the Maxim and the Riviera and the Dunes, and everywhere I worked I saw who got special treatment—relatives, friends, golf buddies, pretty women, and dope dealers. I'm not exaggerating when I say that some dealers never dealt a hand unless they were high. High was their norm. One day I'm on break, and I go into the men's room to take a leak. I decide to use the stall instead of the urinal. I'm about to flush when two people come in. I recognize the pitboss's voice right off. He's asking if it's pure, and the guy who ends up being a dealer on the other craps crew says he'll prove it. I stood up on the toilet and watched as they went over to the sink, which has a faux marble countertop.

The dealer shakes some white powder out on the counter and then takes out an eye dropper. He sprinkles a drop from the bottle on the powder, which turns this really blue, like a robin's egg only deeper. He looks at the boss and says, "Never doubt a professional," just like he's goddamn James Bond the drug chemist or something. Someone told me later that the liquid is cobalt something or other.

I get to thinking about the position I'm in. I crouch down so they won't notice me. They talk a little bit. I hear them snort some, turn on the water, dry their hands, and then they leave. I wait a few seconds before I flush the commode. Outside, I stop to check my watch. The dealer is sitting on a bench looking at me. We trade nods. He knows that I know.

The next break the boss comes up to me and starts talking like we're the best of friends. He never before talked to me so friendly. I want to play dumb, but I can't. I look up at the ceiling as he's talking. I'm playing it cool. I tell him I saw them in the men's room, but it's none of my business. He nods and says if I ever need anything, to come see him. That was the Dunes. They blew it up, and now the Bellagio is where it used to be. The boss, I don't know what happened to him, but the dealer's a big man in one of the casinos now, a top host. I can't say where.

1980-84

Years ago at the Maxim I worked with a married couple who seemed ideally suited to one another. They worked the same shift, both of them read, they liked wine, smoked a little grass, shared the same friends and an almost identical sense of humor. They'd met in Reno while working in a casino and later moved to Las Vegas, where the money was better. They pooled their money, paid off a house in five years, and saved another fifty thousand besides so that they could get out of the business. They were diligent, never wavered, never missed work unless deathly ill.

We used to go to parties at their house, just a few of us, an intimate group. We gossiped and trashed the casino, told stories, ate, and generally had a good time. The last party held at their place was to celebrate their quitting. They'd bought a trailer park in Washington somewhere near the coast and were headed up to live the good life. They'd earned it. The rest of us were jealous. They'd done what all of us wanted to do—get out. We toasted their success.

They sold the house and left in the spring with enough reserve money to keep them going for a year or more, even if the trailer park didn't pay the way. We talked about them after they were gone until they'd become almost legendary. Gone. Made the break. The big escape.

It was six months later that we got word that the husband was back in Nevada, working at a club in Reno again and that the wife had taken on a lover some ten years younger than she was. She'd met him in a mental ward where he had worked as an orderly. She had admitted herself for alcoholism and depression. Everyone speculated about what had happened to them. I got the husband's phone number from information in Reno and called.

"It was like what had kept us together was gone," he said and explained how once they'd accomplished their goal, they didn't know what to do next. She had always been a binge drinker, he admitted, but up there with nothing else to do, the booze took control of her.

"Isn't it funny? The thing we hated the most, the casino business, is what kept us together. We thought we loved each other, but the truth is we just hated what we were doing. Oh, I love her, but like a sister now."

He said that his coming back to the casino was ironic, but the truth is he didn't hate it so much now that he wasn't with her. I never told the other dealers that I called him. One of them was close to the wife and had gotten another rendition of the split-up. It didn't matter. The story had a sad ending any way you looked at it.

1992

One day these two middle-aged men sit down at my game and fill the last two seats. They both buy in with hundred-dollar bills and start playing. I don't pay much attention. The circumstances are ordinary, and the table's full, and I'm too busy to pay a lot of attention. After a few hands, I realize that this one guy, the taller of the two, hasn't lost a hand. He lays his bet down, plays basic strategy, and signals for a hit or to stay, always with his left hand. Nothing unusual, except that he can't lose. And it keeps going that way. Before it's all over, he's won about a thousand dollars.

He stands up to leave without tipping anything. I shouldn't have said anything, but I did. I honestly wasn't even trying to get a toke out of him; it was that he had just had about the longest winning streak without a loss that I'd ever seen, and I had to comment on it. I clear my throat until he looks.

"Sir, you didn't lose a hand."

"What's that?" he says kind of loud so everyone would hear.

I figure I've offended him except it wasn't intentional, so I repeat myself in a much softer voice, "Sir, you didn't lose a hand."

"What's that you say?" he asked.

He didn't seem angry or anything but was looking at me in a strange way, almost smirking. Now everyone at the table was involved, waiting to see if he was going to complain or something. I figured it was best just to get it over with so I could deal the next hand.

"Sir, I simply said that you didn't lose a hand."

"Then what the hell am I doing with this thing?" He smiled and set his right hand on the table.

It was a prosthesis complete with rubber skin and fingers that moved. He wiggled the fingers for me, and when he did I lost it. I was laughing so hard that the boss came over to see what was so funny. The man tossed me two five-dollar chips and said that it was for laughing. He must have waited for years to pull that on some dealer.

1993

One day four of us were working a string on two roulette wheels at Harrah's, one on break, two dealing the wheels, one mucker. For an hour I was mucking checks and racking them for another dealer. He'd been in the business about three years. I didn't know him well, but he seemed easygoing enough most of the time. This particular round he was dealing to four people who bet fifty-cent chips. It was a slow game. The other table was dead, so I was helping him even though he didn't need help. No one was tipping, and the players were ahead of the game, as we say. All in all, no one was betting very much, two and three chips straight up and approximately the same on the splits, corners, and streets. It wasn't a game that attracts any attention from the bosses.

The dealer's cheeks were red, and he muttered occasionally under his breath as he cut out payoffs. On one occasion I pushed him the exact payout for two chips straight up on the number. He left my stacks and instead cut out another payoff. I thought I'd offended him or something. Then I noticed that when he lined the stacks up to pay the bet, he shorted the player. I didn't say anything, just kept my eyes on the layout. He spun the ball, and when it landed, he marked the number and swept the layout, following procedure step by step. He obviously knew what he was doing. Again he shorted the players by a few chips. This went on for several more spins. Finally, he noticed that I'd spotted him pushing out short stacks.

He winked. "Stiffs, the whole table."

Two more times during the shift I had to muck checks for him. Both times he shorted the players, except for one who was tipping. I didn't say anything to him or snitch on him.

About a week later I was in a similar string, working the same wheels. The dealer I spoke of before shorted the players again. I guess by then he thought I was in on it. I was uncomfortable with him doing this, but what could I do? This table was busier than the one I'd been on with him the week before, busy enough that the boss looked over now and then. That fact didn't seem to bother the dealer at all. He shorted the players despite being watched.

Later the business in the casino slowed down, and his game was closed. He and I caught a break together. He sat down across from me in a booth and sipped coffee out of a mug. I didn't say anything about what I'd seen. It was up to him to bring it up. In time he set the coffee mug down, leaned over the table, and said, "I see you hate stiffs as much as I do."

I said no one likes stiffs and let it go at that.

He was fired a week or so later. No one knew why. I figured it out but said nothing.

The job is difficult, and players are annoying sometimes, but stiffs are part of the scene. They bet their money, take their chances, and contribute to keeping the casino doors open. Hell, if all the stiffs were run out of the joints, the casinos would be about half the size they are now with about half as many employees.

I never cheated a player, never gave it a second thought. It's wrong, and it sure isn't worth losing a job over and risking being arrested by Gaming Control agents. But I guess the dealer I'm talking about couldn't take it, the monotony of paying off winners time after time and them never tipping. It's hard to figure his thinking. Maybe he thought he was solving something, you know, making his world right in some small way.

UNDATED

I work every day. Got a wife and kids. People say this isn't a rewarding profession. Well, it's bought me a damn nice house and boat that I take my family out on. We've got more than many people. Part of the problem, I think, is with the idea that dealing's a profession. Law is a profession. Medicine is a profession. So are teaching and banking and accounting. Dealing is a trade. We've got to look at it just like anybody out there pouring cement or pounding nails does that job. You do the work, and you earn a wage. That's the reward.

Too many people I work with can't accept that concept. I don't know what they want, but they won't find it behind a layout. Maybe we'd all be better off if the casinos got rid of tipping, and we had a union. Pay us by the hour, and let us bargain for our wage and benefits. That way when we punch in we'd know that our labor has begun. Eight hours of work and regular wage. Isn't that what most Americans do? Take the tipping away and give the job a little dignity. That's the solution. There's nothing in the world wrong with working for a paycheck.

You want to get rid of the bitching because some winner stiffed the dealers? I'll tell you how. Pay us starting at eighteen an hour and scale it up to twenty-five. Dealers will be a hell of a lot more friendly to players when they don't have to live off generosity. It's not such a radical idea, but it will never play in the casinos. They don't want to pay anything. Talk about having it made. Pay minimum wage and build, build, build. I don't resent them. I'd do the same if I could build a casino for two hundred million and pay minimum-wage scale to my employees. Then I could build onto the hotel and expand the casino and sell it off for five hundred million. It's business.

But the dealers don't fight for anything. I was around when the Sahara voted for the union. The election was certified, everything legal. What happened? Court appeals, delays, dealers fired or laid off. Was a contract ever bargained for or signed? No. Dealers! Let them bitch. They deserve their lot. Take the money home to a family and do the best you can. It's a trade. Nothing professional about it.

7

GAMBLING

When customers asked me if I gambled, I used to say to them, "What kind of work do you do?" The responses were varied—insurance, car sales, homemaker. I'd respond with something to the effect of: "When you're not cleaning your own home, do you go next door and clean your neighbor's?" Or, "When you're not selling a policy, do you go listen to someone else make a sales pitch?" The last thing I wanted to do after an eight-hour shift in a casino was go into another casino or a bar or anywhere noisy and smoky. I was forever amazed by the number of dealers who left work and went out to gamble.

Some dealers I worked with ended up spending a day's tokes on the nearest slot machine. Others preferred the table games. Still others bet the horses or sporting events. A few couldn't wait to leave work. In the dealers' room at the Maxim there was invariably a game of tonk or pitch going on. It wasn't unusual to see one or two dealers lose a day's tips in a game of one- and two-dollar pitch. I worked in six different casinos, and in every one of them someone was booking bets on sporting games. A few dealers bet the sports and held back enough money to play cards on breaks.

When I broke in at the Mint in blackjack and roulette, I dealt often to dealers from the Horseshoe, the Golden Nugget, and the Four Queens who were on their fifteen- or twenty-minute breaks. They'd come in with their aprons off, buy in for twenty, and stack chips all over the layout, everything on one spin. Occasionally they'd come in in pairs or small groups and descend on a game like locusts, hands flying all over the place as they laid the bets down. I'd end up mucking up about a thousand chips, win or lose, and if they hit a number, they didn't toke. They'd just give me one of those I'm-stuck-a-bundle looks. Once I had a group from the Four Queens on a roulette game, and they hit the big number, chips stacked all over it. They jumped up and down and hollered, happy as any tourist who'd hit big. They'd been in twice that evening. I knew they were stiff and in a hurry to get back and work. I didn't flinch, just took my time paying each one and pushing the stacks out. They were hollering at me, telling me what the payoffs were, etc. I nodded and moved as unhurriedly as possible and still get the job done. One of them complained to the floorman that I was too slow. I'll never forget what Maury said to them.

"He's got all night to get it right."

Maury smiled at me and walked away.

It didn't take long to learn to pick out the degenerates, the ones who have lost control of their lives. They'd sit on the game, living and dying with every spin, every toss, every turn of the cards, losing more than they could afford. Whether another dealer or just a customer, a sadness surrounded them, a kind of infectious doom that sat almost as heavily on me as it did them. I could never gamble, be like them, because for a given time I was a unwilling witness to their despair. I didn't want any of my own. A dealer once said to me, "If everyone's here for a good time, why isn't anyone smiling?"

I think the major reason why I never took up gambling was that type of experience, that being an unwilling party to someone else's misery, and I simply didn't want to impose myself on some other dealer or to see in a dealer's eye that knowing look. It's as if we all should know better. But too many didn't and don't. Some have lost cars and houses and jobs and wives and husbands, everything to gambling.

1999

It went on for over forty-five years before I ever came out here, first sports, mostly football and baseball. When I came out here, I'd go bet a game or two. Next thing I was hanging out and playing keno. You don't want to know how much I blew. Hundreds of thousands. What's strange is that even though I was a dealer I never had any interest in the table games. It was always keno until video poker came out. Then it was both of them. My wife never knew. No one ever knew. It was a regular thing, too. I'd hit the nearest joint when my shift was up. A couple of tickets, maybe more at first. This goes back to the early sixties.

It's not like I don't know better. I saw chump after chump lose his shirt. I know the odds. I was an accountant back in New York. Got a degree. When I came out here, I got on dealing. Carl Cohen was my cousin, and he put me to work at the Sands, which was the best job in the state. It was easy, and the money was five times what I was used to as an accountant. Now accountants make the big money, but not then. I was making so much. Two hundred a day wasn't unusual. I took care of business then because I had kids at home. Sent three of them through college. One's an attorney now. It really got crazy after they were all on their own. I was still at the Sands. It had gone to hell as far as money goes, but my habit stayed the same. I just couldn't back off. I was playing keno less and less but hitting the slots in stores. I hit a big keno ticket, over sixty thousand, and paid off all my debts. That should have been it for me, but no. Before a year was up I blew my life's savings, every penny, and had the house, which had been paid off, mortgaged to the hilt.

My wife never knew. It got so bad that I had to tell her. All those years, all the saving for retirement. It was the hardest thing I ever did. I mean I love my wife, never even looked at another woman, and I had to tell her. Once I did, I knew I could start helping myself. I've been going to Gamblers Anonymous. It hasn't been long, but I tell everyone I know. I want them to know so that I won't go back. It helps, too. I think I can make it. I have to. I can't think of the money. It's gone, and I have to accept that. But I do wonder how it got hold of me. I'm a smart man, don't drink, never chased around, always knew the value of a dollar. It was just bigger than me. Doesn't matter if you know the odds. It's that feeling that gets hold of you. Inside. You know what I mean?

UNDATED

I'm way ahead. The last two months I've hit four royal flushes. I'm lucky. I never go in more than twenty-five dollars. A drink or two when I'm playing. It takes the edge off a day. Some nights I lose, but I don't chase it. I'm lucky.

UNDATED

I worked at the Sands forty-two years. When they shut the doors to blow it up, I knew I'd never work in a casino again. I didn't have to. I took care of my money. I was never a gambler or a drinker. And I have family. That's what kept me on top of things. Anyhow, there were dealers from the old days who left there with nothing. A few of them were players. It's a sickness. Some of them were driving Mercedes and taking vacations to Hawaii in the old days, but they walked out with nothing. All that money we made! It's sad. One of them is essentially homeless, living off Social Security, most of which he gambles. Imagine. I saw him. I didn't know what to say. That's how you end up if you don't look out for yourself. Maybe someone should start a home for retired dealers. Instead of charging they could just put on a few slot machines and a couple of blackjack tables.

8

ONE DEALER'S STORY

When I first sat down with this dealer, most of what is in this book was already in place. I was expecting, as I had from the others, an anecdote or a story or two to add to the text. He'd been dealing for approximately fifteen years, more than enough time to accumulate a reserve of stories. I had worked with him a few years earlier and had known him casually. He was known as a nice guy to take a break with, bright, sometimes witty, and good at safe small talk. He could get a bit moody from time to time. Perhaps even then what I was sensing in those moods was suppressed anger. It's hard to say. What I hoped for when I asked him for a story was something unique, something a bit bizarre or humorous to include in the book. I got far more than I expected.

He and I sat across from one another at a table in a Borders bookstore, me with coffee in front of me and my pen and paper ready to take notes, him with an iced tea held in his hand, drinking slowly and looking at me as if he'd made a serious decision. He said that he'd thought about it, about what he wanted to say, and decided that the story he wanted to tell was his story. I told him okay. He nodded and began.

My pen never touched the paper. I listened. He talked. It was the most candid, most compelling personal story I'd ever heard. It was like listening to the confession of a killer who was trying to understand why he killed. But the difference was that all the transgressions he'd committed were against himself. That first session he talked for an hour and a half, nonstop. His story contained in many ways the essence of what I hoped to capture in this book.

1989–2000

I was raised in this town, came here when I was in elementary school. After I graduated I went to work for the Nevada Power Company. It was an easy job, and I got along with my bosses and my fellow workers. I never thought about going in casinos, never gambled. At the worst I'd have a few drinks. I was twenty-nine and had lived here twenty-two years. At the time I was living with a roommate who dealt blackjack at the Desert Inn. Every two weeks he'd bring home two thousand dollars in tips. I was making about twenty-seven thousand a year at the power company. It didn't take much to figure out that he was doubling what I brought in.

I figured (and it didn't take much brain power) that if I stayed at the same job I'd never make that kind of money, so I quit and learned how to deal blackjack. The first job I got, about fifteen years ago, was at the Gold Coast. It was an off-the-Strip casino with a lot of local trade. I remember my audition. I was nervous, didn't do very well. The whole experience was pretty scary, and I figured I'd blown it. I got off the game, and the boss who'd auditioned me said that I "could shuffle." It was kind of funny. I got the job.

The worst thing was dealing to money. I'm not talking about a lot of money like the players bet on the Strip, but twenty-five and a hundred dollars. It was terrible going in on those games. My hands would get clammy and shake, and I'd perspire so bad I could feel it trickle down my sides. But I wasn't the only one sweating. The bosses sweated the money pretty bad, not really sweat but worry. If I lost any amount of money, the bosses wouldn't talk to me when I came off the game, but if I won they'd look at me with an expression that said "good job." It didn't take long for me to get the message: A good dealer was one who won. Some nights when I was a "bad" dealer, I'd get punished for it. You know, in subtle ways. No one ever came up and said I was a bad dealer. Just a look or a shaking of the head. Then I'd end up on a two-dollar-minimum game for the next two weeks.

They just wanted you to win. It didn't matter how you dealt the game, how neat or fast you were. In fact, sometimes the bosses would say things like "slow down." But if you were winning, it was "speed it up," you know, bust the player. Some would even say things like "Go in there and get the money," as if it were possible to control the game that way.

I felt the pressure and wanted to please the bosses. At my other job my bosses had always been friendly. We worked like a team. This was different. I was afraid of the bosses, afraid of their power, so I went in the game and tried my hardest to deal fast. But the money always scared me.

In time I got to know a lot of the players. You'd see the same ones night in, night out. It was like their home. One woman had inherited a good-sized fortune from her husband, some kind of businessman who'd died wealthy. We watched her blow that money. Someone told me it was way over a million, maybe two. I can't be sure, but it was a lot of dough. It was sad in its own way. Here was a woman who had it made for the rest of her life. Now she works, had to get a job to feed herself and her habit. She still goes into the Gold Coast. Crazy.

After a while I got better at dealing, at least mechanically. I was fast and accurate and learned roulette and baccarat as well. The bosses took to me a little more, you know, stand by the game and shoot the breeze. And I got to know the dealers. Eventually I started dating one. She was a night person and liked the swing shift routine, etc. We moved in together. I started drinking when I got off work—in casinos. I don't know how it began, but not long after I was making lay-downs, betting it up if I won. I had some runs, too. Here I was watching players bet a hundred or more a hand and winning once in a while, hitting a streak, and when they didn't walk away, I'd think they were chumps. I didn't have that kind of money, but I was going out and betting after work like I did have it. I didn't tell my girlfriend, either.

All you would ever make as a dealer at the Gold Coast was an envelope that averaged about sixty a night or so. I was building up debt, you know, going to shylocks and loan companies, paying outrageous interest. The only way to improve my finances at the Gold Coast was to go on the floor as a game supervisor. So I did. This was even more boring than dealing. And it seemed like no matter where I went, the games I watched ended up losing. It was amazing, but the casino seemed to hold me personally responsible, like I wasn't doing my job or something. It was crazy. Soon enough I found myself saying things like "I lost a lot tonight," as if I were responsible. Mostly my job entailed making sure the game moved along and was on the square. I had other responsibilities, like tracking players and making fills. I did what I was supposed to do. Still, the bosses over me made me feel like I was responsible. I was unlucky, a label that followed me.

In the meantime I was still gambling and drinking. I can't remember when the drugs entered the picture, but they were part of the scene. I got involved with blow. It took over my life. Next thing I know, I'm tooting it at work on my break, etc. I kept this from my girlfriend as well. I was feeling the whole strain of everything in my guts. One of my duties included counting the number of decks in my section of the pit when I came on. I had to write down the total and sign my name on a sheet. This one night I count them, and the figure is ninety-eight when it's supposed to be one hundred. So, I counted again. This time I counted a hundred. That's what I wrote down and signed for. If there was any discrepancy, I was supposed to call the boss. Well, I didn't. A boss from the previous shift had used two decks and wrote a note to that effect. So, his figures, which were in conflict with mine, were noted by the shift boss. I was called aside and chewed out, not admonished or corrected, but called every kind of name and told I'd be sent back to dealing two-dollar games for the rest of my life. A chewing-out wasn't uncommon for him, but he went overboard for a small issue such as this. He didn't just ream me out once but came back later and did the same thing, both times in front of witnesses. I was humiliated. I started hating him and my job.

A couple of years later I landed a job dealing at Harrah's. I stayed clean and passed the drug test. I was making a hell of a lot more money. I bought a Cadillac, a used one that was cherry as hell. I felt like the treatment there was amazing compared to what I was used to. I was told that if I had a problem, I was to bring it to the boss's attention, meaning the pitboss or shift boss. I didn't have any trouble for a long while, then one shift when I was dealing roulette, the floor person, a guy who'd started out years before as a casino porter and worked his way into a dealing and later a supervisor's position, got all over me, not because I was dealing wrong but because I was losing. He wanted his pets in the pit and no one else. He dressed me down in front of the players while the game was going on. It was humiliating. The players were distressed. They wanted to know what his problem was.

I thought about it and decided to complain. I went to the pitboss. Little did I know that he and the other supervisors were good friends. I was told that it would be handled. Later I was pulled into the craps pit by the shift boss, who told me that the only way matters could be settled was if I apologized to the floorman. I said that was ridiculous. The shift boss started screaming at me. He threatened me with my job, etc. I knew I was in the right. I'd done nothing wrong and had followed the instructions I was given when I went to work there. The shift boss told me that the supervisor had forgotten more than I would ever know about dealing roulette. He threatened me again and browbeat me into submission. I agreed to apologize.

Once again I was disillusioned. I went along to get along.

It was around this time that I started thinking I wanted a family, a normal life. My girlfriend, however, wasn't all that interested in having kids. I was working day shift; she was on swing at the Stardust. She liked the night-shift style, the kind of wild openness that casino employees on nights engage in, not that she was wild, but it was just more exciting than day shift. And there were more characters on swing shift. This is about the time the cocaine really took over.

This guy at Harrah's would front me the dope, and I'd pay him when I could. Every shift my envelope was going out for something. I was still gambling, hoping, I guess, for some score to get me squared up. But that didn't happen. I was still borrowing money and hocking things even. I was making over a hundred and fifty a day and had nothing. I lost the Cadillac and my girlfriend. I rode a bicycle to work. No one ever raised an issue about why. Here I was making all that money and using a bike to get to and from work, and no one seemed to see something was wrong.

By then I was pretty hip to the insides of casinos, and Harrah's was pretty much like the others, except that here several of the bosses, who'll go nameless, were into cocaine, etc. I mean the very bosses who should have noticed I was using. Hell, they knew. The thing is if you're on the ins with them, there will never be a problem, just don't put them in jeopardy in any way. The guy who was my supplier was taking care of them as well. Of course, they could afford a habit a lot more than I could.

I wanted to get straight, clean everything up. I was starting to bottom out when Harrah's was laying off dealers. I didn't want to be one of those let go. The job was all I had. I went to the new shift boss and laid it on the line, said I had a drug problem and wanted to get straight. The insurance had a setup with a drug rehab center with follow-up outpatient service. I went in.

I started the program. It was supposed to be kept confidential, but it wasn't. I came to work and, no matter what, dummied up and dealt. I was serious about cleaning up. Though I didn't gamble, I did slide once. I mean, my supplier was right there offering to front it to me. Finally, I was headed in the right direction, so I didn't buy any more. I got myself on a plan to pay off my debts.

I completed the first part and was attending the follow-up sessions, doing well, when I was called aside and told I was being let go. Jesus, I wanted to punch someone. I know that one of the reasons I was picked was admitting my problem. There were others who had similar problems but kept their mouths shut. The boss told me that I could still finish the drug program. I did.

I wish it had worked right away the first time, but it didn't. Rehabilitating a habit isn't all that easy. I was depressed. My girlfriend and I were breaking up, living separately. I slipped. I applied at a couple of places and flunked the drug tests. I was desperate, financially, at the end. I hated to do it, but I went back to work for the Gaughan casinos, the New Orleans. I hadn't been using the weeks right before applying and did all the tricks, bleaching hair and all, for the drug test. They put me to work dealing the action games because of my experience. I was coping a lot better, kept my head down and dummied up and dealt.

Then one day the boss calls me in and says they have to let me go. I blew the drug test.

I went through some serious depression. It just seemed like this huge hole had opened up and swallowed me. I hated casinos and blamed them for all my problems. It was easier that way.

Then one day I had an unexpected surprise, a sort of miracle, really. This woman I was renting my room from was cutting my hair, which she used to do for a living. As we're talking, I revealed bits about myself that she rightfully recognized as indicators that I needed help. She encouraged me to talk about my troubles, which, of course, I was blaming on everything and everyone but myself. She had me figured out. Eventually, she told me that she had been a substance abuse counselor. I could tell she cared, that she wanted to help. Once the problem was in the open, it didn't take long for me to admit my problem. She encouraged me in the right direction to find help.

I started attending meetings with this organization, where I've found the kind of help that I needed, and I found a job as a waiter. In time I was able to begin work on clearing up my debts and get a car, but what was more important was that I felt better about myself. It took quite a while, but finally I quit drugs, quit gambling, but I'm not cured exactly, just working on an ongoing process that keeps me from relapsing. I didn't experience what you would call a miraculous change but more a slow, steady climb out of that hole, which in a way is a greater kind of miracle. Now I'm working in a casino again, but I know the pitfalls and how to avoid them. It's up to me. I'm not going to lay the blame on the casinos any longer. That's just not at all true. We have choices, but I'll be the first to say the joints provide an atmosphere that promotes gambling and drug and alcohol abuse. It's in your face all the time if you're weak enough to jump into it. I'm looking to get out of the business now. I'm not exactly sure what I'm looking for, but I'm looking and preparing myself for the day. I beat the worst of it and now know there's opportunity out there. If I look for it, I'll find it. Until then, I just dummy up and deal.

SOME AFTERTHOUGHTS ON THE TEXT

Experience itself tends toward disorder, leading us from a point uncertain to another point that was not necessarily predictable. The purpose of a narrative is to give order to the experience and lead the reader to a point that is ironically called the truth of the story. This *truth* is found in experience reduced or expanded through language to an ultimate effect, from which it can best be deduced that there is no absolute knowledge in human experience, that every experience is relative to contrasting experiences and subordinate to the variables of language and, thus, subject to explication. The proper narrative guides without giving direction, informs without commentary.

These stories and anecdotes are, no matter how shaped, true to memory, and memory seeks its own fact in each retelling of a story. Some are accounts of my own experiences behind a table, but most incidents described here came directly to me from the lips of dealers in informal interviews or were passed across the tables in cafeterias or break rooms where dealers played cards, drank coffee, and smoked and told the stories that define their subculture. A very small number are stories passed around much like folklore. I made no distinctions between my experiences and those of other dealers. At the outset, I had, it seemed to me, two options: to identify each and every source or to keep each and every one anonymous. Some dealers feared retribution. Others simply desired anonymity. I gave thanks by name to those who contributed and wished to be mentioned. Their motives for wishing that their stories be told are as varied and as similar as the stories they tell. Some characters in these pages are composites, and many of the voices are inventions to facilitate transcribing spoken language into a more readable, more lyrical form or sometimes to add some nuance to their stories. That which is invented is used merely to augment the telling and not to distort the fact of the matter. Although I opted not to reveal the tellers' identities, in some instances I have included names of notable gaming figures integral to the story—Billy Douglas, Harry Goodhart, Frank Rosenthal, Bob Stupak, Carl Cohen, and Benny Binion, for example. Not to name them would do a disservice to the intent of this book and the kind of truth these stories capture. Some of what is written here is obscured by time. Who exactly told me a particular story eighteen years ago seems as irrelevant as the name of a specific soldier who fought in the Battle of the Marne. It is enough to know that a soldier fought and lived or died. It is his contribution to the big battle that interests historians; it is who he was within the context of his experience that the creative writer wishes to explore.

GLOSSARY

agent. An outside man or woman, usually the one who takes the chips or brings in the fixed deck or dice in a cheating scam.

ballsy. A term applied to a player who will bet big and usually against the odds.

bank. The rack of chips in front of the dealer from which he or she pays the players; also, a row of slot machines.

bend. To bend cards in a deck so that their denominations can be discerned by a skilled cheater.

big-six. A large upright wheel with spokes, sprockets, and a clapper that is spun by hand by a dealer. Its stops are marked by bills ranging from one dollar to twenty dollars and two forty-to-one signs. The big-six is often referred to as the "wheel of fortune" by laypersons.

bird game. A low-minimum game, usually the closest to the entrance, designed to attract players passing by or leaving a casino.

blackjack. A card game wherein the hand closest to twenty-one wins after all hands have been played out; a combination of a ten-value card and an ace that pays three to two.

blacks. One-hundred-dollar chips.

break-in. A novice dealer; also a rookie.

bust or bust out. To go over twenty-one on a blackjack hand.

button. Another term for a lammer; a small pad soaked with daub (rouge paint), usually disguised or hidden, which is used to mark up a deck of cards.

cage. The room where the casino keeps cash to pay players for chips and reserve money and stores chips when not on table games.

call bet. A bet announced by a dealer and acknowledged by a supervisor; a courtesy bet extended to a player, the amount being marked by a lammer button. Call bets are common on all games but roulette and usually not allowed there.

checks. Casino chips.

chipmunk. A dealer who steals chips by hiding them in his or her mouth.

clap out. The action of clearing hands and showing open palms when a dealer leaves a game.

clerk. At one time an accepted term for a dealer; a complimentary title for a good dealer.

cooler or cold deck. A deck that is set up for the players to win and is usually handed to the dealer in a switch of decks during a cutting of the cards.

count. To keep track of the number of ten-value cards and aces in a deck by using a running plus-and-minus system; a once-each-shift accounting of the chips on the table games. (It is by calculating this and the drop plus the credit slips minus the fill slips that the winning percentage on a given shift is determined.)

credit line. The amount of credit extended to a player who has verified his or her ability to pay back the amount advanced in house checks.

credit slip. The slip that goes into the drop box when a player pays off a marker or chips from the game are returned to the casino cage.

cross roader. A cheater.

crossfire. The act of dealers talking to each other on games; commonly frowned upon by management because the dealers are not paying full attention to the layout or to players.

croupier. A European and British name for a dealer, not used to describe dealers in Nevada casinos.

daub. The coloring (noun) or act (verb), when referring to a deck marked with rouge or ink.

dead wood. A term once applied to discards that went to the bottom of the deck. This gave deuce dealers a chance to roll the deck (called "rolling the dead wood") before hitting a hand and thus use a card to the house's advantage.

dealing deuces. Dealing the second card from the top.

degenerate. A term usually applied to habitual gamblers, especially those who demonstrate other compulsive and often offensive behaviors.

deuce dealer. A card dealer who deals seconds; a mechanic or house man.

discard rack. An open plastic shelf, usually red, where used cards from the deck are stored until it is time to shuffle.

drop. Buy-in money from a player and/or credit slips.

drop box. The box on a game where money is secured. Such a box is changed at the start of each shift in a casino.

early out or EO. The last break of the shift, which allows a dealer to leave work twenty to thirty minutes early.

envelope. The term for the dealer's tips for the day; derived from the fact that dealers' tips usually are sealed in an envelope. ("Living from envelope to envelope" would mean day to day.)

eye in the sky. Surveillance operatives who watch from above, looking for cheating activity or rules violations; applies to camera surveillance as well.

fill. Checks brought to a game to resupply the bank or rack of chips.

fill slip. The paper that records the amount of a fill on a given game. It must be signed by the person making the fill, the person bringing the fill, a supervisor, and a dealer. The signed copy is dropped in the drop box.

fire. A table that is on a losing streak; as in "There's a fire that needs putting out."

fireman. A house man or woman skilled at cheating who is called in to put out fires (house losing streaks).

flat house. A casino that employs any one of a number of methods to cheat players.

flats. Dice that have been shaved to give the house or the player an advantage.

flea. The worst kind of degenerate player; flea as in pest.

floorman. See *floor person.*

floor person. The immediate game supervisor. Normally one floor person supervises three to five blackjack games or one to two craps tables.

front man. A boss (one who can hold a license) under whose license a casino operates; usually a front man for the Mob.

George. A tipper, one who is considered generous with money.

greens. Twenty-five-dollar chips.

Griffin Investigations. A private agency that is commissioned by the casinos to watch for cheaters and cheating activities. The agency maintains a book of mugshots of suspected cheaters.

hand mucker. One who brings cards into a game and switches them as a hand is being played.

hand switch. The act of switching one or both cards from one player to another.

headliner. A marquee-name entertainer, such as Frank Sinatra, Wayne Newton, or Elvis Presley.

high roller. A big bettor.

hit. To take a card on a blackjack hand.

hole card. The card under the dealer's up card in blackjack.

hot streak. A winning streak.

house. A casino.

hustle. The acts of dealers working to get bets for the house or tips for themselves from players. (The house desires the hustling of bets in favor of the house but discourages the hustling of players for tips. There are two kinds of hustles: the hard hustle, which is sometimes called "muscling," and the soft hustle, which is less overt and requires finesse.)

joint. A casino.

juice. Influence or favoritism somewhat akin to nepotism or cronyism; to mark up or fix a deck with paint. To "juice in" means "to fix."

key employee. Usually a shift boss or above in the rank of casino executives. This employee's license must be approved through a hearing of the Gaming Control Board after a background check confirms suitability.

lammer. The button placed on the table layout to indicate the amount of a call bet.

lammister. Person on the run from a past life, from the law, or from a problem such as failure to provide child support.

layoff. Money from tips given to a boss who either helps dealers make tips or looks the other way when dealers are hustling.

lay off. The act of terminating a person from employment, usually without cause (as opposed to firing).

lump. A bad or clumsy dealer.

marker. A signed note of debt endorsed by a player against his or her credit line, resembles a counter check.

max or maximum. The highest amount allowed as a bet on a given table or in a given casino; amounts vary from casino to casino.

minimum. The lowest amount allowed for a bet on a given game.

muck. To pick up and stack chips in roulette (from a term for cleaning out animals stalls and slag from mines; thus a dirty job); to cheat a game by removing a card and replacing it with another.

mucker. A dealer who gathers up, separates, and stacks chips by color or denomination; a cheater who uses a device or a gypsy move to conceal a card in his palm as he exchanges it for a house card.

paint. To mark up a deck.

paint man. One skilled at marking cards.

past-post. To lay a bet down on a winner after the dice have rolled a point in craps or the ball has dropped on a number in roulette. (The expression comes from the racetrack, where at one time bets were laid at the cage illegally after the horses reached the post, thus finishing the race.)

pat hand. In blackjack, a hand that needs not be hit, usually a hard seventeen or above.

pit. A section of gaming tables. (Tables are usually organized in patterns based on the types of games, as in "blackjack pit," "craps pit," and "baccarat pit.")

pitboss. The person on a given shift who supervises a casino pit. Normally there are two or three in smaller casinos (one each for baccarat, craps, and blackjack), but in larger casinos there may be one for each pit.

player. When said with emphasis, means one who will fire money at the house.

proposition bets. On a craps game, the bets such as the hard ways, the seven and eleven, and the craps on the layout in front of and between the stick man and the box man, also called "props." (The house expects the dealer to hustle these bets because they highly favor the house odds.)

reds. Five-dollar chips.

roll. A winning streak; a hand on the craps table.

rounder. One who distracts the dealer's and boss's attention to enable someone else to cheat a game or slot machine; someone who drinks and gambles regularly and excessively.

sand. A speck of sandpaper glued to a fingertip. The sand is used to mark up a deck.

shift boss. One who is in charge of the casino operations on a given shift. This person answers to the casino manager or assistant casino manager.

shot. The act of a player trying to take advantage of a dealer or the house, as in "that degenerate took another shot at me."

shylock. A person who lends money at usurious rates.

snapper. A blackjack.

soft hand. Any combination of cards in blackjack that along with an ace can be hit without busting: an ace and a five would be a soft sixteen; an ace and a seven would be a soft eighteen. (Downtown casinos require that a blackjack dealer hit a soft seventeen.)

spin. A hand on a roulette wheel.

spin and mic. The act of measuring and balancing dice to make certain they are true. A related technique is to drop a die numerous time into a glass of soda water to determine its random fall.

stick. The instrument used to move the dice on a craps game, also called the "mop."

stick man. The dealer moving the dice with the stick and calling and placing proposition bets.

stiff. A hand that is breakable; a player who does not tip.

store. A casino. (A "good store" is a casino where the dealers earn good tips or are treated particularly well.)

sweaters. Bosses and dealers who worry about losing the house's money.

tap out. The act of one dealer relieving another from a game.

toke. A tip.

whack-out dealer. A card mechanic who is trained to beat players by employing cheating skills, such as switching hole cards and dealing seconds.